Today's sports world is heading out of bounds. There is too much showmanship and not enough sportsmanship. What's missing is Christian character between the lines of competition. This book is a great resource to help you become the athlete and teammate God designed you to be.

> Les Steckel
> President, Fellowship of Christian Athletes

Winning the Super Bowl was great. And being a NASCAR owner has been wonderful. But neither of those accomplishments eclipses the joy of knowing Christ. I encourage athletes and coaches alike to Get in the Game *for a true spiritual workout.*

> Joe Gibbs
> Coach Washington Redskins

Every aspiring athlete should read this book by Dr. Tony Evans and his son Jonathan Evans. Having coached for 37 years and now spend every day of my life working with coaches, I clearly understand the value of clear and precise advice that will make each student a more rounded individual. After all, we are all physical, mental, and spiritual.

> Grant Taft
> Executive Director, The American Football Association

This book is a book of life that talks about not only my athletic life but also my spiritual life, which is the most important thing.

> Herschel Walker
> All-Pro NFL running back

Get in the Game *is a practical training guide for athletes young and old to get and keep their spiritual lives on track, so that they can live a victorious Christian life.*

> Tony Dorsett
> Dallas Cowboys

Dr. Tony Evans and his son Jonathan have given athletes an excellent and exciting training tool for maximizing their spiritual potential and growing deeper in their walk with God.

> Avery Johnson
> Coach, Dallas Mavericks

Get in the Game *takes athletic illustrations and examples and applies them to the Christian life. Whether you're a world-class athlete or just a casual sports fan, you'll relate to the way that spiritual principles are outlined in this book.*

Tony Dungy
Coach, Indianapolis Colts

*Athletes who want to expand and grow in their faith will benefit from reading Pastor Evans' newest book—*Get in the Game. *It cites numerous real life examples that all athletes can relate to, revealing the importance of a relationship between religion and athletics. The unique exercises following each chapter will help readers grow.* Get in the Game *shows how having a strong personal faith helps athletes excel in the use of their God-given talents both on and off the playing field. It's a real spiritual workout and I heartily recommend it.*

Roger Staubach
NFL Hall of Fame, Dallas Cowboy quarterback

Every serious athlete knows that good conditioning is essential to success on the playing field. Good conditioning is even more critical when it comes to living a successful life.

In Get in the Game *my good friend Tony Evans and his son Jonathan have given us an excellent spiritual conditioning program to enable athletes to live a victorious Christian life.*

Mike Singletary
NFL Hall of Fame, Chicago Bears
Assistant Head Coach, San Francisco 49ers

An Athlete's Guide for the
Spiritual Journey

GET in the GAME

TONY EVANS
& JONATHAN EVANS

WITH DILLON BURROUGHS

MOODY PUBLISHERS
CHICAGO

Cover Designer: David Uttley | The DesignWorks Group, Inc.
www.thedesignworksgroup.com
Editor: Pam Pugh

Library of Congress Cataloging-in-Publication Data

Evans, Anthony T.
    Get in the game : a spiritual workout for athletes / by Tony Evans and Jonathan Evans with Dillon Burroughs.
        p. cm.
    ISBN-13: 978-0-8024-4406-6
    1. Athletes—Religious life. 2. Sports—Religious aspects—Christianity. I. Evans, Jonathan, 1981- II. Burroughs, Dillon. III. Title.

BV4596.A8E93 2006
248.8'8—dc22

                                                                2006012354

ISBN: 0-8024-4406-7
ISBN-13: 978-0-8024-4406-6

We hope you enjoy this book from Moody Publishers. Our goal is to provide high-quality, thought-provoking books and products that connect truth to your real needs and challenges. For more information on other books and products written and produced from a biblical perspective, go to www.moodypublishers.com or write to:

Moody Publishers
820 N. LaSalle Boulevard
Chicago, IL 60610

1 3 5 7 9 10 8 6 4 2

Printed in the United States of America

This book is gratefully dedicated to my good friend Bob Breunig whose love for the Lord and for sports has resulted in great impact for the Kingdom of God as well as for my national ministry.

contents

how to use this guide

The goal of *Get in the Game* is simple: you will discover truth directly relevant to living for Christ in the athletic world. This interactive workbook serves as an ideal tool for personal learning, team & coach devotions, group discussions, and church curriculum.

Personal Learning: Utilize the information and takeaways for your one-on-one times with God to provide direction for your own spiritual journey.

Team and Coach Devotions: It can be intimidating to prepare spiritual material to share with teammates or with the team you coach. Instead of trying to come up with your own material, choose a portion to read and a couple of quotes or questions to challenge your team. The end of each chapter also includes material specifically for use by a coach.

Group Discussions: Ideally, this material's applications will be multiplied as you discuss it together with friends, roommates, teammates, family members, or other friends in an informal setting.

Church Curriculum: When your church group needs a resource that offers decisive truth for today's issues, this workbook will provide real answers, stimulating discussion questions, and challenging takeaways for action.

the pre-game

T hirty minutes until kickoff. The sportscasters begin, sharing the strengths and weaknesses of each team, the statistics of the previous week, the star players, the key stories, and the legendary rivalries. Sound bites play, drums roll, players take the field. The National Anthem. The coin toss. The opening kickoff. The game has begun.

Days, weeks, months, even years have been invested in preparation for the upcoming moment—the very instant when practice becomes performance and role-playing becomes reality. Sweat, blood, and tears will be evident as opponents seek their spot in the ongoing story of sport. Another day in the life of the athlete.

Regardless of your sport, whether football, baseball, swimming, volleyball, hockey, or something else, one thing remains the same—to win, *you must get in the game*. No amount of practice or preparation provides victory without the moment of truth when the plays drawn on paper become the collisions and jolts experienced on the field.

While this may seem obvious to an athlete, many athletes miss the critical spiritual parallel their sport represents. While God may change our lives *apart* from our works, He still expects our greatest efforts in our pursuit of Him. Too many Christian athletes are content to be on the team or watch as a fan rather than get in the game of living out an authentic Christian faith.

For those who are not sure of their faith in Christ, please know that this must be your starting point. This means agreeing with God that you are a sinner and unable to make yourself right with God by your own efforts. Then you must believe that Jesus Christ died on the cross for you personally and place your trust in Him alone as your Savior. Once you trust Christ for the free gift of eternal life, you are in the game and ready to begin the journey of living a productive and victorious Christian life. Don't turn another page without accepting the challenge to follow Jesus using a personal prayer similar to the following:

"Jesus, I know I am a sinner and in need of Your forgiveness. I believe You died on the cross and rose from the dead to give me eternal life. I now receive that gift and trust You alone as my sin-bearer. Teach me how to follow You as my Lord."

It is our prayer that the words of these pages will motivate, inspire, and assist you in the challenge of getting in the game for Christ. While each sport has its top championship that every athlete dreams of winning, the journey of following Christ provides an eternal win beyond what we could ever imagine. May you be strengthened in your reading and learning, both on your own and with your teammates, as you pursue to get in the game of passionately following Christ.

symbol of demonstrating this death and resurrection through the tradition of baptism.

In Romans 6:3–4 we read, "Do you not know that all of us who have been baptized into Christ Jesus have been baptized into His death? Therefore we have been buried with Him through baptism into death, so that as Christ was raised from the dead through the glory of the Father, so we too might walk in newness of life." Baptism is not salvation, but it is a public picture of what Jesus did for us. When we are placed in water at baptism, we are picturing our identification with Christ in His death. As we emerge from the water, we declare our identification with Christ in His resurrection.

One day at football practice my (Jonathan's) coach taught me a new blocking technique. It wasn't natural for me; as a matter of fact I was terrible at it. It seemed that the harder I tried, the worse I performed. One day my coach told me that the ability I needed to be successful at the technique was already in me. I just needed to stop trying so hard and let what was in me show. He was right! When I followed his advice, I excelled at the very area that had been a great weakness.

> Christ wants to give you everything you need to grow and live to be more like Him.

Living the Christian life is the same way. We know it is very difficult to maintain the walk to which God has called us. It seems the harder we try the worse it gets. We sometimes hear the comment "I'm just a sinner saved by grace." This is only partially true. We are new creations in Christ who *continue to struggle* with various sins in this life. A Christian should not say, "I am a homosexual" or "I'm a slacker," but, "I am a new person in Jesus Christ who is struggling with the sin of homosexuality or with self-discipline." If you define who you are by what you do, you confuse identity with performance. Knowing who you are in Christ completely changes your reference point.

Paul takes it a step further, writing, "We have the mind of Christ"

(1 Corinthians 2:16). We now have the capacity to think God-like thoughts. This new mind also includes our emotions, desires, attitudes, and all of the other components that make up the core of our being.

Finally, we also have a new location. When Christ raised us from the dead, He raised us all the way. After Christ was resurrected, He ascended back into heaven and is seated "at [God's] right hand in the heavenly places" (Ephesians 1:20). If our identity is bound up in Christ, guess where it leads? We are also seated "with Him in the heavenly places" (Ephesians 2:6). That's a spiritual reality, not just wishful thinking. Everything that happened to Christ in His death, burial, and resurrection happened to us spiritually.

➤ *What are some ways you have seen people confuse their identity in Christ with their performance for Christ? How does this actually hurt our spiritual lives?*

The Reborn Supremacy

Our identification with Christ is complete: "It is no longer I who live, but *Christ lives in me*." What a powerful phrase! Something supernatural happens to our soul as we come to know Jesus Christ.

The most essential truth of the spiritual life is that Jesus Christ is in us when we trust in Him. Yet Galatians 2:20 takes this concept much deeper, promising that Christ is both in us and is living through us.

1. Home-field advantage

The difference between these two is the difference between our unchanging standing in Christ and our ever-changing state in Christ. Ephesians 1:13 shares that we are "sealed in Him with the Holy Spirit of promise." This is His seal of security no one can break and that guarantees us heaven.

But Christ wants to do much more than promise us heaven. He longs to live in us—to move in and fully express Himself through our lives. Sadly, many believers headed for heaven are not maturing on earth because they refuse to allow Christ full control in their lives. They treat Christ the way we treat guests.

We invite our guests to make themselves at home, but we don't usually mean it. We don't want them roaming around the house, looking through our personal files, and eating whatever they want from the kitchen.

It's the difference between living and being alive. Jesus says, "I want to express the power of My supernatural life through your life. I want to live in you." The Bible says, "We have this treasure in earthen vessels, so that the surpassing greatness of the power will be of God" (2 Corinthians 4:7). The purpose of everything we experience is that "the life of Jesus also may be manifested in our body" (verse 10).

▶ *When was a time you remember feeling the importance of the home-field advantage during one of your games? How does having Christ at home within us provide an advantage for our spiritual lives?*

2. You can't do it on your own!

Trying to live the Christian life in your own strength is like wishing we play like Allen Iverson does on the basketball court. If Iverson wrote a book about how to split defenders and shoot three-pointers, you could read and practice every detail in order to perform at his level. Would you suddenly play at his level? Of course not! Why? Because even with the information, we cannot copy the person of Allen Iverson through our basketball skills.

Let's pretend, however, that Iverson would be able to claim, "I am going to enter your body and use your hands and legs to score just like me." Then the situation would be different. With Iverson, this is fiction; with Christ, this is reality. He wants to give you everything you need to grow and live to be more like Him.

In 1 Corinthians 1:30 Paul wrote, "By [God's] doing you are in Christ Jesus, who became to us wisdom from God, and righteousness and sanctification, and redemption." In other words, when we received Christ we gained everything. He is our reborn identity. As Philippians 4:13 words it, "I can do all things through Him who strengthens me."

▶ *What is discouraging about not being able to live a Christlike life on our own? What is encouraging about it?*

The Reborn Ultimatum

The third section of Galatians 2:20 provides the practical application for this reborn life. We have the ultimate example through Christ: "And the life which I now live in the flesh I live by faith in the Son of God, who loved me and gave Himself up for me."

1. The caffeinated Christian life

What is a caffeinated Christian life? The opposite of "letting go and letting God," the caffeinated Christian life is a high-energy pursuit to live the life of Christ by faith. A lot of times we sit around thinking, "God, I know You want me to read the Bible. I'm just waiting for You to give me a real desire to do it." There's nothing wrong with praying for a desire to learn God's Word, but it is more likely to happen when you turn off the TV and actually open your Bible. God is probably not going to levitate your Bible onto your lap and open it to the place He wants you to read. We must work in cooperation with Christ's work in us.

A person who has been using drugs for years may need other people to help him overcome his addiction. Even then, when he turns over every part of his life "as instruments of righteousness to God" (Romans 6:13), he will find new power to break the destructive addiction. Christ can provide all of the needed power, but not apart from our mind and will.

➤ *In what areas of your Christian life do you most tend to "let go and let God"? What is an area where you need to concentrate to live out your faith with passion?*

2. The credible Christian life

Our lives must also offer credibility. Many of us have been carrying around spiritual fake IDs for so long we have trouble remembering who we really are. Whether through our private list of rights and wrongs, an "it's all good" attitude about life, or hiding a personal sin, our tendency is to cover up anything in our lives that does not make us look good.

While there are definitely things we should and should not be doing, it's helpful to learn that we will continue to struggle with sin even as new creations in Christ. Paul, as one of the top early church leaders, revealed his personal struggles by saying he still acted in ways he knew he should not be living (Romans 7:15). Paul had to come to grips with the fact that it wasn't him trying his best to obey God, but it was Christ in him that gave him power to overcome sin (Romans 8:10–11).

> *Why do people try to obtain and use fake IDs? How is this similar to how some people try to live their Christian life? What is an area of life you prefer to cover up because it does not make you look good?*

3. The centered Christian life

Maybe you're ready now, thinking, "I want Christ to live in and through me, but how do I do it?" The answer is found in a centered Christian life, a life focused on the phrase found in Galatians 2:20 that says we live this new life "by faith in the Son of God."

There is no recipe or easy formula for accomplishing this superhuman task. The centered Christian life is a life of faith from start to finish. A reformation was launched four hundred years ago when Martin Luther read that "the righteousness of God is revealed from faith to faith; as it is written, 'But the righteous man shall live by faith'" (Romans 1:17). We live "from faith to faith," from one level of faith to the next.

Faith is not just believing in God, but believing God when He says we cannot live like Him apart from Him. Paul learned that the only way he was going to make it was to tell Jesus, "I can't live this life by myself. I need You to live through me."

The centered Christian life is lived by faith in Christ, but not a cold, academic faith. Galatians 2:20 also reminds us that Christ "loved me and gave Himself up for me." That's the language of a loving, intimate relationship. Jesus wants you to trust Him, but not the way you trust your bank to take care of your money or trust your car to complete your commute. Living by faith is cultivating a relationship with the living Christ who wants you to identify with Him so completely that there is no question as to who is your life (Colossians 3:4).

As followers of Christ, we are totally forgiven, fully accepted, absolutely loved children of God. This is our new identity in Jesus Christ. As we understand our new role in Christ, we can pursue the glorious goal of Christlike living and soar to new heights of spiritual growth.

➤ *Name a person who has lived as a strong example of spiritual strength for you. What did he or she do that made them such a glowing reflection of Christ? What would you like to do that is similar?*

takeaway

You must know your role to reach your goal. (We have a new identity in Christ that redefines our roles and goals in this life and *for eternity.)*

training points

What parts of your new identity in Christ do you find the most difficult living out in daily life? For example, do you often struggle to believe you can now overcome a major sin area in life because Christ lives in you? Write down your thoughts to share with the group and to reflect on during the upcoming week.

1. _____

2. _____

3. _____

transforming others

Who can I tell about my new identity in Christ? What is a specific way I can communicate my new life with them?

What group of people could I best have an impact on based on my past experiences and how Christ has changed me since? Where is one place I can begin in connecting with this group of people, even beginning with just one person?

the coach's perspective

Ask your players, "How do you want to be remembered?" As an optional exercise, have each person write an obituary, telling how he or she would like to be remembered after their time on earth is over.

"Like newborn babes, long for the pure milk of the word,

that by it you may grow in respect to salvation."

—1 PETER 2:2

FULL-COURT PRESS

(THE ATHLETE AND COMMITMENT)

God desires full-court followers of Christ.

I n basketball, there are two basic approaches to playing defense: half-court or full-court. Most of the time teams play half-court defense, allowing the offense to bring the ball within about thirty feet of the basket before seriously defending every move. Full-court defense is just the opposite. Every pass is challenged, every dribble cut off, every action contested at top intensity. Full-court defense is generally only used when a team falls far behind or during the final minutes of a game. Yet some teams choose a full-court press at other times to throw off the opponent or to gain an edge in order to win.

God desires full-court followers of Christ.

Too many who claim to follow Jesus today are content to react only when absolutely necessary rather than with an everyday intensity that brings advantage and victory. However, our spiritual journey requires our total commitment.

Peter confronted this issue long ago with the words, "Like newborn babes, long for the pure milk of the word, that by it you may grow in respect to salvation" (1 Peter 2:2). A newborn infant wakes at all hours, cries frequently, and requires full attention from its parents. Parents tolerate such behavior knowing that 3:00 a.m. feedings will not last forever. If human parents show such concern regarding their children, then it should not surprise us that our heavenly Father does as well.

Before discovering what a full-court follower of Christ is, let's first discuss what it is not.

What a Full-Court Follower of Christ Is Not

1. **A full-court follower of Christ is not just someone who knows the Bible**

Some people view spiritual growth primarily through the accumulation of Bible facts. They believe growth will automatically follow if you attend enough Christian seminars, read enough books, gather enough information, and study the Bible enough.

It would be similar to an athlete who studied all the rules of the game, yet never played the actual game. Could someone who had read fifty books on surfing be able to dive into the ocean and instantly compete with professionals in the sport?

While this may seem comical to us, this is exactly what Jesus claimed was true of the spiritual leaders of His time. He challenged them by saying, "You search the Scriptures because you think that in them you have eternal life; it is these that testify about Me; and you are unwilling to come to Me so that you may have life" (John 5:39–40).

These men knew the facts. They were the religious scholars of their day, but they did not believe in Jesus. They remain an example today showing we can know all the right answers, yet still not personally know God.

➤ *When is a time you knew how to do something in theory but had trouble actually doing it when the time came? (For example, as a springboard diver you may be able to explain how to perform a particular dive, but executing it is a much different thing.)*

2. **A full-court follower of Christ is not just someone following the rules**

Others think that spiritual growth comes from following a particular set of rules. They want to know the ten steps to maturity or the five factors to faithfulness. Lists of steps are often helpful, but you can follow all the steps and still not reach spiritual maturity.

This does not mean there are not clear stages of growth or processes that help, but such a mechanical approach cannot guarantee spiritual development.

> *Have you experienced a time when you felt like you were just going through the motions spiritually? What were the "motions" you continued to follow? Why were these motions not enough to help you feel strong spiritually?*

3. **A full-court follower of Christ is not someone who just avoids things**

A third misconception about the nature of spiritual growth is the belief that abstaining makes someone more spiritual. While most people in our culture are extremely action-oriented, there are some who think it is more spiritual to withdraw from nearly everything. This includes those who require that people devoted to their religion abstain from certain foods or from marriage, who condemn holidays, or who mistreat their bodies in order to discipline themselves spiritually.

This approach to spiritual growth is historically known as asceticism. It began with some aspects of monastic living (but not all) and reached at times to include even the most bizarre behaviors, such as people whipping themselves or sitting on a high pole in solitude for years at a time. Imagine someone sitting on a billboard for three years to grow spiritually! This is

some think spiritual growth comes from following a set of rules.

exactly the kind of behavior some have attempted in order to grow closer to God.

Unfortunately, such self-denial ultimately fails to produce lasting growth. Wrong desires come from *within* our hearts, something no form of self-denial can remove. There's nothing wrong with avoiding evil influences, of course, but discontinuing wrong habits is ineffective in itself unless these are replaced with Christlike activities resulting in spiritual maturity.

It's vital to discover the true marks of a full-court follower of Christ.

Through God's truth, we can learn the positive ingredients essential to our spiritual development.

The Marks of a Full-Court Follower of Christ

1. Identifies spiritual growth as a necessity

First, it is necessary to recognize that spiritual growth is not optional; it is God's requirement. The consequence of not growing is to become spiritually out of shape. Becoming a full-court follower of Christ is not a choice—it is a command.

When talking about becoming a full-court follower of Christ, we're really just talking about growing spiritually. It's the process of allowing God to transform us from the inside out.

John the Baptist said it best. His followers noticed the growing popularity of Jesus and asked, "Do you realize what's going on here?" (John 3:22–26). John responded, "He must increase, but I must decrease" (verse 30). We are growing spiritually when more of Jesus is being expressed through our lives.

➤ *What are some specific ways you can make Jesus increase in your life?*

2. Pursues spiritual growth with a passion

If you have ever heard a newborn baby cry out for food, you can appreciate the apostle Peter's words of encouragement: "Like newborn babies, long for the pure milk of the word, so that by it you may grow in respect to salvation" (1 Peter 2:2). This is the best one-sentence description of spiritual growth you will find in the Bible. We may not know exactly how spiritual growth works, but this verse helps us because it compares spiritual growth to physical growth. Just as an athlete trains to develop physically, Peter describes the vital importance of developing ourselves spiritually.

In this verse, the issue for a newborn baby is physical development leading to maturity. This may seem so simple and obvious that you wonder why it is mentioned. However, the importance of intentional spiritual growth is often overlooked. Becoming a full-court follower of Christ is ultimately not a program but a passion to become what Jesus desires for your life.

> *On a scale of 1 to 10, what is your current passion for spiritual growth? Why do you think this is true in your life?*

3. Views spiritual growth as a relationship

A baby is dependent on other people for the nourishment needed to grow. This demands a relationship that begins even before birth as an unborn child draws nourishment from the mother through the umbilical cord. In this case, the importance of that relationship is clear because the baby is feeding from the mother, who is supplying life to the child. If that relationship is disrupted, the baby is in serious trouble.

It's interesting that Jesus did not say, "I have come to give you My program," but, "I came that they may have life, and have it abundantly" (John 10:10). So if we are not growing as we should, even though Jesus came to give us not just life but abundant life, then maybe it's because we have punted our relationship with Him or traded it for something less. Spiritual growth is progressively learning to let Christ live His life through us. This only happens through a relationship.

> *What are some common things (e.g., habits) people often pursue in place of Christ? How do these replacements fail to satisfy spiritually?*

Starting Points to Becoming a Full-Court Follower of Christ

Again, Peter's voice rings out clearly on this issue: "Grow in the grace and knowledge of our Lord and Savior Jesus Christ" (2 Peter 3:18).

1. God's part—grace

"As you have received Christ Jesus the Lord, so walk in Him" (Colossians 2:6).

Grace is all that God is free to do for us based on the work of Jesus Christ on our behalf. It is God's endless supply of goodness where He does for us what we could never do for ourselves. Grace is a mighty force that enables us to live lives pleasing to God (Titus 2:11–12).

➤ *How would you define grace? If you are in a group setting, what similar patterns emerged from each of your personal definitions?*

We can see why grace is required for spiritual growth. Spiritually dead people cannot grow. The law of the Old Testament could only point out the sins of humanity but could never remove them completely. That's why Peter said if we are going to grow, it has to be by grace. Grace is not just the prayer we offer before a meal; it is the foundation for our life in Christ, since it enables us to experience all that God has given us at salvation.

2. Our part—knowledge of Jesus Christ

Professional football players invest hours each week viewing game footage of upcoming opponents. Players strive to gain every possible competitive advantage through a thorough knowledge of their rival.

The same emphasis on study is critical for our spiritual growth. We must know what God wants us to do but also know the God who wants us to do it. It is a knowledge that includes both understanding and personal relationship.

➤ *As an athlete, how do you prepare for an upcoming game or competition? What parallels do you see from your sport that would be helpful in your spiritual habits?*

What Happens When You Become a Full-Court Follower of Christ

Looking back again at 2 Peter 3:18, notice the ending words: "To Him be the glory, both now and to the day of eternity." God takes His glory very seriously. Check out these two aspects of God's glory that assist us in becoming full-court followers of Christ.

1. **You were created to bring God glory**

Becoming a full-court follower of Christ ultimately results in expanding and increasing our capacity to bring God glory. God exists for *His* glory! It is not all about us. Recognizing this will revolutionize our entire approach and attitude toward spiritual maturity.

Many Christians are not growing, even though they desire a closer relationship with Christ. The problem is often that their emphasis is on them and what *they* are doing, instead of focusing on God. God said He created people for His glory (Isaiah 43:7). This issue is so important that the Bible defines sin as a failure to bring God glory. "All have sinned and fall short of the glory of God" (Romans 3:23). That means we are not sinners merely because we do wrong things, but because in our sin we fail to honor God.

The word *glory* meant to be "heavy" or "weighty" in the Bible's original language. It came to refer to something or someone of great worth. When we glorify God, we are saying He is a person of great value. We attach weight or importance to Him. Glory also has to do with the way that something attracts attention by the way it shines. Glorifying God means we draw attention to Him and promote Him as worthy of all praise. God is invisible, but He has created people whose full-time job is to make Him visible so the world will see God through them.

➤ *"Glorifying God" is often used in very vague ways today. What are some specific ways you can really glorify God with your life?*

2. **Glorifying God must be your passion**

Glorifying God is a radical decision and passion to live for God's honor. Once you decide you are going to be consumed with God's glory, your entire life will be pointed in a new direction. It's like putting on a pair of tinted glasses that colors everything you see. First Corinthians 10:31 puts it this way: "Whether, then, you eat or drink or whatever you do, do all to the glory of God." God is passionate about His glory, and spiritual growth increases our capacity to bring God glory.

One reason this commitment is so radical is that it is the direct opposite of the way many people view God today, even the way they are taught in some churches. Many people treat God as a vending machine that gives us what we want when we make our selection, drop in our quarters, and push the right button. It's easy to live as though God were here to glorify us, fulfillimg our desires and longings upon request.

God is certainly not against blessing us. However, this is the overflow of our decision to live for Christ. Don't forget that God's blessing may also include extreme trials and problems we would never choose for ourselves. Our greatest growth often comes during our times of greatest struggle.

If you *are* pursuing a relationship with Jesus Christ and are passionately committed to bringing Him glory, your spiritual life will grow at a speed you never imagined possible. Your growth will take care of itself as you feed your soul on God and His Word, the way a child's growth takes care of itself as he feeds and exercises his body.

We often say to a child we haven't seen in a while, "My, just look how you've grown!" That child's growth is evident to everyone because he has out-grown his clothes and his old shoes no longer fit. That's what will happen when you are pursuing Christ and His glory. Your growth will be evident to everyone. People will say, "My, look how he's grown!" They will be attracted to you and discover that God is the focus and glory of your life. The reason so many Christians aren't growing as they should is that God isn't getting the glory He deserves from their lives. God only honors that which honors Him.

➤ *How do you see people using God as a vending machine for their own desires? In what ways have you noticed this tendency in your life?*

The Results of Living as a Full-Court Follower of Christ

1. **God will bless your life**

Peter told Jesus, "We have left our own homes and followed You" (Luke 18:28). In other words, Peter wanted to know, "What's in it for us?" Jesus didn't criticize Peter for asking. He simply responded, "Truly I say to you, there is no one who has left house or wife or brothers or parents or children, for the sake of the kingdom of God, who will not receive many times as much at this time and in the age to come, eternal life" (verses 29–30).

➤ *How have you experienced God's blessing in your life as a result of following Him?*

2. **God will change your life**

Second Corinthians 3:13 tells us that Moses had to wrap a veil over his face so God's people would not see the glory fading away from his being in God's presence. Paul relates this story to our lives today by saying, "But we all, with unveiled face, beholding as in a mirror the glory of the Lord, are being *transformed* into the same image from glory to glory, just as from the Lord, the Spirit" (verse 18, italics added).

➤ *In what areas have you encountered God changing your life recently? Be specific and share one personal story if studying this material in a group setting.*

Romans 8:28 promises that God causes all things to work for the good of those who love Him. That's a promise, but don't miss the purpose God gives us in the next verse: "For those whom He foreknew, He also predestined *to become conformed to the image of His Son*" (verse 29, italics added).

God is constantly working to make us more like Christ. He wants us to grow even on our most difficult days and during the worst situations. If you pursue becoming a full-court follower of Christ, God will take care of the results and allow you to enjoy your spiritual life to its fullest.

takeaway

Growing in Christ requires pursuing Christ. (Remember, God desires full-court followers of Christ!)

training points

What major steps do you want to take in becoming a full-court follower of Christ this week? Write them down below and share them with your learning group.

4. _____

5. _____

6. _____

transforming others

Who can I help grow in the knowledge of Christ this week? How will I do this?

What will I do this week to share my love for Christ with someone else?

the coach's perspective

Ask your players, "What would you consider to be ultimate commitment as a player on our team?" Listen to how they describe practice habits, attitude, and character. As an exercise, have each player list their top ten character traits for a model team player. Afterward, discuss how this is also the expectation for us as believers, not to check off a list, but to set an example by our level of commitment.

"Our old self was crucified with Him."

—ROMANS 6:6

FOULING OUT

(THE ATHLETE AND SIN)

There are always consequences when you break the rules.

Shaquille O'Neal towers over even many of the NBA's tallest players. At seven feet one inch tall, 340 pounds, few can compete with him inside the lane. Try as they may, often the only strategy for containing this living legend is through committing fouls.

It has become known to his opponents that his area of weakness is not his slam dunk but his free throw. However, to send Shaq to the line requires an illegal move—a foul—in order to gain the advantage.

This same principle is often seen in our spiritual lives. We may recognize early in life that the easiest way to get ahead seems to be doing something that is not allowed. Maybe you've caught yourself saying, "Yes, I ran four laps," when only three were completed. It may have been, "I didn't do it," when in fact you did. Students often cheat on an exam because they think that it is a quicker and easier way to score a high grade and pass the class.

Whatever the reason, the root of such actions is what the Bible calls sin, and it's very common. In fact, Scripture claims that all have sinned and fall short of God's glory (Romans 3:23). In other words, we've all fouled out spiritually. Until a new game begins (another opportunity), we are stuck on the bench.

Sin's impact on our lives is not accidental. The Bible in its wisdom reveals three giant spiritual opponents. These include the world (an evil system, 1 John 5:19); the flesh (our evil desires, Romans 7:14–15); and the Devil (an evil person, Revelation 12:9). They join forces in a well-executed game plan to use sin to defeat our spiritual growth. Yet we are not defenseless, because Jesus has victory over the world (see John 16:33; 1 John 4:4), God has given us victory over our evil desires (see Romans 7:25), and God has defeated the Devil through Jesus' death on the cross (see Hebrews 2:14).

> *Tell about a time you committed a "foul" spiritually that seemed unimportant at the time but that you knew was wrong. How did you try to justify your actions?*

What Happens When We Foul Out

While we have all "fouled out" spiritually, there is an important distinction to make. The sin that stunts spiritual maturity in followers of Christ is not the same as the sin that separates unbelievers from God. The difference between these two conditions is the difference between heaven and hell, but it's also important to recognize that sin separates us from God whether we are talking about eternal separation in hell or the breakdown of intimacy between Christ and His children. Here are two lessons we can learn from spiritually fouling out as believers:

1. We're still on the team

It's important to remember that just because we foul out it doesn't mean we are thrown out. Our relationship with God is eternally settled the moment we place our faith in Christ. Paul wrote, "Therefore, having been justified by faith, we have peace with God through our Lord Jesus Christ" (Romans 5:1). In the same chapter, Paul said that through the sacrificial death of Christ on the cross, we have been "made righteous" (verse 19).

Justification in the New Testament was used as a legal term that meant to be made right. When we come to Christ for forgiveness, God charges our sin to Christ's account and credits our account, making us right. This allows God to declare us as righteous because we are *in* Christ.

Paul also describes it this way: "He made Him who knew no sin to be sin on our behalf, so that we might become the righteousness of God in Him" (2 Corinthians 5:21). This is the ultimate exchange of our sin for access to enter heaven.

If you have not trusted Christ for salvation, you have already been convicted as guilty of sin by God. There is nothing you can do to earn your freedom. You may put in hours of community service, be involved in many spiritual activities or show kindness to others, but there is no sufficient human payment available for your sins.

we've all fouled out spiritually—until a new game comes along, we're stuck on the bench.

When you come to Jesus Christ for forgiveness of sins, they are forgiven completely. You are made right with God forever. As part of the transaction, God provides a new life that requires development and growth, just as a beginning athlete requires much practice before excelling in his or her sport.

> *Briefly share your spiritual background. How did you come to trust in Christ by faith? For those unclear on this issue, take some time to discuss and pray together regarding a faith relationship with Jesus Christ.*

2. We're still required to work hard

How many times have you heard a follower of Christ say he wished he didn't have to continue fighting against sin? The day is coming when Jesus will deliver us from sin's power and even its very presence. Until then, however, we must deal with sin, but we have a powerful teammate in God's grace. As grace flows to us and through us, it trains our new nature, the new one God has placed in us.

John said, "No one who is born of God practices sin, because His seed abides in him; and he cannot sin, because he is born of God" (1 John 3:9). But how can we avoid sinning when sin confronts us every day? Don't misunderstand this verse. It is "His seed," the new attitude God placed in us, that cannot sin. It is impossible for anything that comes from God to sin in any way. His spiritual DNA has no defects. Your new nature is without flaw, so your new nature cannot sin.

"Our old self was crucified with [Christ]," Paul tells us (Romans 6:6). We still fight against sin, but it no longer has full control of our lives. The good news is that the new nature is now in the dominant place of influence and control. As long as we are in our human bodies, sin will continue to be a problem. Our new nature exists in our earthly flesh, and they are in direct competition with each other.

That's why the Bible says, "The flesh sets its desire against the Spirit, and the Spirit against the flesh" (Galatians 5:17). One way to know you are saved is that you feel this spiritual battle going on inside of you. Unbelievers don't have this battle because they are controlled by sin and do not have the Holy Spirit. That's why it's so important that we grow in Christ. The more we grow, the more the Spirit controls rather than our sinful desires.

➤ *When was a time you felt discouraged at your failure to control your sinful thoughts? What are some specific ways you can fight against these thoughts in the future?*

How to Spot a Foul

Have you ever found yourself wondering how that referee could possibly have made such a call? We often criticize those who call the fouls or penalties in our games, but the truth is that they have one of the most difficult tasks on the field. Spotting sins is no different. It's easy to spot sin in someone else's life, but we are often blind to the fouls we commit in our own lives. John provides some insightful wisdom on how to spot a foul and what to do about it as we seek to keep from fouling out in our walk with Christ.

1. It's against the rules

First John 1:5 says, "This is the message we have heard from Him and announce to you, that God is Light, and in Him there is no darkness at all."

When "light" is used of God in the Bible, it stands for His absolute holiness and purity. No darkness, sin, or evil can exist in the perfect light of God's presence. Sin is anything that is against His rules or His ways.

The easiest way to spot a foul is to watch for anything against God's rules. God's rules, of course, are the principles found in the Bible. John wanted us to understand the complete contrast between the God of light and the darkness of sin, so he added the phrase, "In Him there is *no darkness at all*." God is telling us that He will never change the rules because of our situation. In terms of our intimate connection with God, if known sin is present in our lives and remains unconfessed, our relationship with Him has been damaged. We have committed a foul.

> *What are some of the most common fouls or penalties in your main sport? Common fouls are often the most difficult to avoid, and the same is true regarding sin. What are some of the most common sins you notice people repeating in daily life?*

2. Don't get used to it

In basketball, commentators often speak about referees calling a close game or whether they "let the players play." Sometimes it seems the action is so rough that what would normally be called a foul is disregarded and only "hard fouls" are called. Even on the playground, you hear the phrase, "No blood, no foul."

Unfortunately, this same tendency can also happen to us spiritually. We must remember that God doesn't view sin that way. He has one standard, and John tells us that sin cuts us off from fellowship with God. When this happens, we have committed a foul and the game is stopped. We must continue to play within His guidelines so our relationship with Christ will remain vibrant and strong.

> *Describe a game or competition you have played in where fouls or penalties have stopped your momentum. What are some spiritual momentum killers you have noticed in your life?*

(Be honest and specific. These can include what you watch on television, your language, dating relationships, and much more. The more willing you are to share, the more open others will be to share about their lives.)

3. **It's the opposite of the right style of playing**

Did you notice the contrast implied in 1 John 1:5? John spells it out in verse 6 just in case we missed it: "If we say that we have fellowship with Him and yet walk in the darkness, we lie and do not practice the truth." If we say we are close with God but also allow sin to exist unchecked in our lives, we are living a lie.

By definition a foul in basketball is simply any infraction or breaking of the rules. It's the opposite of the way a player should be playing. The same is true in this passage from John. If our lives contradict God's standard, we have committed a foul. We have sinned.

Verse 7 then continues, "But if we walk in the Light as He Himself is in the Light, we have fellowship with one another, and the blood of Jesus His Son cleanses us from all sin." Please note that the blood of Jesus cleanses us from sin while we are walking in the light. This is because only when we expose our-selves to the light of God's standard through His Word do we see our sin clearly so we can confess it. This exposure allows us to maintain fellowship with God when we respond properly to what the light reveals.

➤ *What do you consider some of the areas God has exposed in your life that need to be addressed? How have these negative qualities hurt your rela-tionship with God?*

Raise Your Hand

When someone commits a foul in basketball, you often immediately see the guilty player raise his hand. While occasionally there is uncertainty about who the call is on, it is usually easiest when the offender admits to it, the foul is reported, and the game continues smoothly.

The same is true of spiritual matters. We have two basic choices when it comes to the sins that cut us off from a close relationship with God: we can cover it or confess it. When we confess or come clean with our sin before God, we have the powerful promise of 1 John 1:9: "If we confess our sins, He is faithful and righteous to forgive us our sins and to cleanse us from all unrighteousness."

This is a comforting truth. This is a verb form in the original language that meant to "keep on cleansing." It is a continual process. The great thing about following Christ is that it is not just for heaven; it works on earth, too. In dealing with our sins, there are some important principles of application that help as we "raise our hand."

1. Admit to it

When basketball players are unwilling to admit to a foul, the game is often delayed as referees confer to decide which player was at fault, excuses are made, and time is wasted. Admitting to the fault simply helps everyone to deal with the situation.

In recent years there have been growing complaints by basketball fans about the whining of players when they are called for a foul. Instead of simply accepting foul calls, players are increasingly arguing their case, pointing fingers, and shaking their heads in disbelief.

When this attitude arises in our spiritual lives, it frustrates our relationship with God and often also with the people around us. The best response is to admit sin as soon as it happens in order to quickly resume play and not lose momentum.

> *Share a time when someone complained to a referee or an umpire about a call in one of your games. What happened that hurt both themselves and the rest of the team?*

2. Agree to it

The word "confess" means to agree or say the same thing. When we confess, we agree with God, saying, "Yes, Lord, I agree that this was sin, and I confess it to You."

Notice that the plural word "sins" occurs twice in 1 John 1:9. The emphasis is on the individual sins we commit, not sin in general. It's tempting in competition to ignore our weaknesses and just say, "We didn't play our best game today." It's much more difficult to actually give the specific reasons we didn't reach our goals.

God wants us to not only admit our wrongs but also specifically agree that the individual wrongs we have done are wrong and in need of change. God doesn't want us just to throw everything together and say, "Oh well, we lost today." The time to confess and be cleansed of a sin is the moment we are aware of it.

> *Think about a game you lost and share what reasons you gave for the loss. What kinds of reasons did you give? Was it easier to give general reasons for the loss or to give the specific factors that resulted in the other team winning?*

3. Remember it

What would happen if your teammate charged into the defensive basketball player and received a charging foul, not once, but three or four consecutive trips down the court? Would you cheer him on, encouraging him to do it again? Of course not! The coach would take the player out of the game. You and your other teammates would literally pull him away to keep it from happening again.

Most people are pretty forgiving the first time we make a mistake, but the same cannot usually be said the third, fourth, or fifth time the same problem occurs. God allows sin in our lives partly so we will remember it enough to not keep doing it. All sin is serious because it disrupts our relationship with God. Confession is designed to help us keep short sin accounts with God so they don't keep happening again and again.

When we confess, God is "faithful and righteous to forgive us our sins."

- *Faithful* means you can trust Him.
- *Righteous* means He won't compromise His integrity.
- *Forgiveness* means that sin is no longer charged against our account.

You can't just rewind the play and not commit the foul during the replay. However, you can remember it. This is the grace of God at work. Confession allows us to keep from repeating sin by triggering God's forgiveness so the flow of grace continues. When grace flows, growth follows.

➤ *What happens to teams that commit a high number of fouls or penalties? What similarities do you see from these observations that apply to our spiritual lives?*

4. Learn from it

While we must confes sins, serious change is necessary for Christians who are living in an ongoing, sinful lifestyle. The Bible calls this "walking like mere men" (1 Corinthians 3:3). In these situations, confession about a sin is not enough. Getting back into the game must include learning from our sins. The result is doing something about it, a concept the Bible calls repentance.

Repentance means to change your mind in order to reverse your direction. It is turning from sin back to God to bring an end to God's discipline for walking in sin. It would be like a player stuck on the bench because of an attitude problem who decides to change his ways in order to return to the starting team.

The prodigal son of Luke 15 is a good example of this process. He had left his family, wasted his inheritance, and was out on the street when he came to his senses regarding his sinful lifestyle. He returned to his father content to simply work as a servant, yet was greeted with a warm embrace and a homecoming party.

God is holy. He will not bless a person who claims to follow Him yet does not live a lifestyle consistent with those claims. We must raise our hand when we commit a foul, quickly jumping back into the game with a diligent effort to learn from our mistakes, and not continue committing them.

Only then can we keep from fouling out from the championship lifestyle God desires for our lives, a life that shines to our teammates and all who are around us.

➤ *When was a time you "blew it" during a game or competition that helped you in the future?*

takeaway

It takes more than one foul to foul out of the game. Learn from your mistakes and keep growing.

training points

What are two or three "fouls" you want to remove from your life? Write them down and discuss ways to help each other become accountable in these areas.

7. _____

8. _____

9. _____

transforming others

Have I wronged someone I need to talk with about asking for forgiveness? If so, what will I do to deal with this situation?

What is the top area I want to change in my life this week? What will I do to keep this area in mind throughout each day?

the coach's perspective

Ask your players, "What key mistakes do we seek to avoid as players and as a team?" As an exercise, use a whiteboard or chalkboard to list these mistakes and the consequences of each. Then ask, "What key mistakes do we seek to avoid as followers of Christ?" List the answers and consequences, helping your athletes see the outcomes of their sinful choices written out.

GIVE IT UP

4

(THE ATHLETE AND GRACE)

You can only win when you lose yourself.

A 250-pound high school sophomore, a star football player, dove from a pontoon boat into Lake Wylie in South Carolina to retrieve a beach ball. The unanchored boat drifted away from him and as an inexperienced swimmer he panicked. A friend tried to save him but was pulled down by the young man's desperate efforts to save himself. If the football player had let himself be rescued, he would have made it. But he never stopped struggling, and he drowned in the 34-foot-deep waters.

Grace only saves you when you stop trying to save yourself. Though many people try to achieve success through their own efforts, the only real way to be saved is through Christ. This is a life-defining issue in which God's Word challenges us to grow (2 Peter 3:18).

Some people think grace is just something to be said before eating a meal, but growing in grace each day involves much more. Grace seems to be such a strange idea to many in today's culture. We live in a performance-based society where people evaluate our statistics, financial worth, job functions, and even our volunteer roles using only numbers, which do not communicate God's full story of grace.

The Bible never commands us to grow in the law. You will never read in God's Word, "Become better rule keepers." Still, living for God and living His way is not an option. Jesus is clear: "If you love Me, you will keep My commandments" (John

14:15). The difference is that our development comes *in response* to God's grace.

One of the clearest pictures of God's grace stands in Ephesians 2:1–10. Paul contrasts what we were like before God's grace with the transformation resulting when grace changed us. Grace allows God to show us His kindness because of what Christ did for us on the cross. As a result, we find that in God's eyes, we only win when we lose ourselves.

Statistics Don't Matter When You Don't Win

Jim Kelly retired as one of the NFL's greatest quarterbacks. He played from 1986 to 1996 with the Buffalo Bills, led his team to four consecutive AFC Championships, threw for over 35,000 yards, was a five-time All-Pro selection, and owns his franchise's records in every throwing category. At the end of his career, however, the thing he remembered most was not his statistics or achievements, but the fact that he never won a Super Bowl, despite making the final game four years in a row.

As Christians we can attend church every service, lead seven Bible studies, serve in nine different ministries, and read the entire Bible three times a year, yet still feel unsatisfied. What matters most in our relationship with Christ is that we remember the sin *from which* God has saved us and the purpose *for which* God has saved us. Sometimes we need to look back and remember where we once were before we can fully appreciate where we are today.

1. Our standing in seasons past

Many athletes dwell on last season's big win for the entire off-season or even for years in the future. God also provided many ways to make sure His people did not forget they were once slaves in Egypt and then lived in the wilderness for forty years.

One of these reminders was during the Feast of Tabernacles (Leviticus 23:33–44). During this one-week celebration, Israelites left their homes and lived in temporary shelters made from branches. When their children asked why the entire country was having a campout, the dad was instructed to tell the story of how God had rescued them from the land of Egypt and provided for them in the desert.

Paul also gained great perspective when reflecting on his life before Christ changed him. He wrote:

> You were dead in your trespasses and sins, in which you formerly walked according to the course of this world, according to the prince of the power of the air, of the spirit that is now working in the sons of disobedience. Among them we too all formerly lived in the lusts of our flesh, indulging the desires of the flesh and of the mind, and were by nature children of wrath, even as the rest. (Ephesians 2:1–3)

In football, receivers often wear black paint under their eyes during night games to help contrast the bright stadium lights when trying to catch a pass. These first three verses of the chapter act as a contrast as well in showing us the evil of our past ways compared to the life we now have in Christ.

Paul summed up our hopeless condition by saying that we were dead in sin. When we begin to reflect and discuss our habits and lifestyle before we were in Christ, we can agree with Paul that these were deadly actions rather than simply bad ideas. While some people have more exciting stories than others from their past, the end result is that we were all losers falling far short of the victory that God's grace provides.

➤ *What was your life like prior to becoming a Christian? What major changes have taken place since beginning your relationship with Christ?*

2. Our statistics in seasons past

Top athletes know that reflecting on past performances can assist in evaluating how to play better in the future. By studying strengths and weaknesses, improvements can be made that will assist in future games.

Paul's report in Ephesians 2:1–3, however, is much worse. He not only said our past performances were poor—he says we were dead! Before we came to Christ, we were cut off from God, the only Source of true life. We were spiritually deceased.

A lot of spiritually dead people don't feel dead. From the outside, they don't even look dead. Yet the Bible clearly teaches that those without Christ are dead in their sins. When we were dead in our sins, we were cut off from the eternal life that Christ gives. Unfortunately, the only alternative to eternal life is eternal death, eternal separation from God and the suffering of hell.

This was our condition prior to the arrival of God's grace in our lives. We were completely unacceptable to God.

> *Why is it difficult to discuss the reality of suffering and hell with people? How does knowing what God's grace provides make His grace even more significant to our lives?*

The Current Standings

The "before" picture of our standing before God reveals a winless season, but there is also an "after" picture. Ephesians 2:4 begins with two of the most important, exciting, and life-changing words in the Bible—"but God." "But God" are words that will reverse any situation. "But God" will bring life where death existed because of what God has done for us in grace.

Follow Paul's thoughts through verses 4 and 5: "But God, being rich in mercy, because of His great love with which He loved us, even when we were dead in our transgressions, made us alive together with Christ (by grace you have been saved)." The last phrase is the key here. Do you understand that if you know Christ, you are saved not because of your decision or anything else you did, but because God took the initiative to reach down and save you by grace? Salvation is God's work from the opening kickoff.

As a person changed by His grace, everything becomes new. These new aspects include:

1. A new team

Toward the trading deadline each season in the NBA, rumors fly regarding which players will be dealt to various teams. Each coach negotiates to guarantee top positioning for the postseason.

As a new creation in Christ, we also become part of a new team with new expectations. Legendary college football coach Lou Holtz put it this way: "I won't accept anything less than the best a player's capable

what does "grace" mean? it means that God has changed the end of our story.

of doing . . . and he has the right to expect the best that I can do for him and the team!" His words of coaching wisdom well reflect the attitude of the new team we belong to in Christ.

Ultimately, grace is God's kindness to us when He could have backed us into a corner as guilty sinners and defeated us without violating His holy character. But God wanted to make us His children. Instead of treating us with the harshness we deserved, He gave His Son over to treatment He didn't deserve, all on our behalf. We now have a new relationship with new teammates because of His grace.

➤ When have you joined a new sport's team? What changes did you encounter? How are these changes similar to the benefits we receive as part of Christ's team of grace-changed believers?

2. A new stadium

One of the most significant transitions in the life of a team is when it begins playing in a new stadium. In 2000, the Dallas Mavericks began their season with the opening of the new state-of-the-art American Airlines Center that stood as arguably the best basketball stadium built to that time. During that year the Mavs set a franchise record for fifty-seven wins in a season and became one of only four teams in the NBA to post consecutive fifty-win records. The team also had thirty-eight sellouts for the season, and surprisingly, even held one of the best road records that year in the league. What made the difference? Many factors helped, but a major strength was the momentum of a new place to call home.

That's what we discover in Ephesians 2. It would have been enough if God had put a period after the tremendous declaration "By grace you have been saved." But grace doesn't stop there. After making us alive with Christ when we were dead, God took us to heaven with Jesus when He rose from the dead and ascended back to His place at God's right hand. As believers, we have something even better than a state-of-the-art stadium. We have a home in heaven with Jesus Christ.

According to Ephesians 2:6, "[God] raised us up with Him, and seated us with Him in the heavenly places in Christ Jesus." There is a divine trading deal involved in grace. God takes the people He has saved and by grace seats them with Christ in what the Bible calls "the heavenly places."

The reality of our lives as Christians is that we are seated with Christ in the heavenly places. This life on earth is just the pregame, not the real game. We have a new location in Christ where all of our blessings are, and we are there by grace.

> *Have you ever played for a team in a new stadium? How did it affect the way you played? How should knowing we have a home in heaven with Christ motivate us today?*

3. A new story

If you think the blessings God has for you today by His grace are wonderful, you haven't seen anything yet. Ephesians 2:7 begins with the words "So that," because Paul is about to tell us *why* God loved us, saved us, raised us up with Christ, and seated us with Him in the heavenly places. God did all of that, "So that in the ages to come He might show the surpassing riches of His grace in kindness toward us in Christ Jesus" (verse 7).

What does this mean? Simply that God has changed the end of our story. No longer are we dead in our sins. In this verse Paul turns from talking about our grace blessings in this present life to those waiting for us in "the ages to come," another term for eternity. Do you know what God is going to spend eternity doing for us? He is going to show us how much He loves us by lavishing His "kindness," His grace, on us.

4. A new lifestyle

The grace of God that brings salvation also transforms us to a whole different way of living. It acts as a powerful force that enables us to say no to sin and yes to righteousness so we increasingly reflect the character of God in our actions and attitudes. Just as a team provides its athletes all they need to perform on the field, even so grace gives us all the provisions to enable us to maximize our spiritual potential (Titus 2:11–15).

What do you look forward to most about your coming home in heaven? How does this new story of life in Christ change your daily focus now?

Living Beyond the Statistics

In Ephesians 2:8–10 we catch a passage that reveals that our story is made up of much more than our statistics. The first part declares, "For by grace you have been saved through faith; and that not of yourselves, it is the gift of God; not as a result of works, so that no one may boast" (verses 8–9). Remember Paul saying that God left the thorn in his flesh to keep him humble? God doesn't want anyone bragging about how he or she earned His favor. You don't brag about a gift someone gives you.

1. Serve out of your love for God

Immediately after this great statement of salvation by faith through grace alone, we read, "For we are His workmanship, created in Christ Jesus for good works, which God prepared beforehand so that we would walk in them" (Ephesians 2:10). Grace should not lead us to try to take advantage of God's goodness by sinning all we want, nor should we serve Him in an attempt to earn His forgiveness. That is working against grace. God wants us to serve Him in response to His relationship with us, a relationship of love and grace.

One time a friend of mine (Tony) was having trouble getting tickets to a Dallas Mavericks basketball game his son wanted to see. So my friend asked a man in his church, whose company is a Mavericks sponsor, if he could tell him where to buy a couple of tickets to the game for him and his son. A week later, this businessman handed my friend an envelope. My friend didn't know exactly what was in the envelope, but when he offered to pay for it the businessman just smiled and told him it was okay. When my friend got home and opened the envelope, he discovered not two, but four tickets to the game. Even better, these were four prime seats costing $135 each, complete with a free parking pass. He took his son and two of his son's college buddies to the game, where they had a great time.

That was a grace gift, but it didn't end there. During the game a Mavericks front office executive walked down to where these guys were sitting and handed each of the three college students a huge bag stuffed with every kind of Mavericks souvenir imaginable, compliments of the businessman who had given them the tickets. My friend said he was completely stunned by the man's generosity. He realized he had no way of paying for this gift. All that he and those guys could do was say thank you and enjoy their superabundant gift.

> *When have you received a grace gift like in the story above? How did it make you feel? How is this similar to what we experience in receiving the grace of God?*

2. Serve out of your relationship with God

Paul said he "labored even more than all of them" (1 Corinthians 15:10), referring to the other apostles, but also added, "Yet not I, but the grace of God with me." Paul knew that he was created in Christ for good works, but his service for the Lord was not a tiresome duty he had to carry out. His goal in everything was to know Christ more intimately (Philippians 3:10). Paul served from a position of relationship, not obligation.

Grace grows by relationship, not by rules. The greater our relationship with Christ, the greater the experience of grace, resulting in greater spiritual growth. On the flip side, grace doesn't mean that we sit back and do nothing while expecting God to do everything. Grace means that we make ourselves available for God to use us.

As many have said, there is nothing we can do to make God love us more and nothing we can do to make God love us less. The more we realize God's grace is all about what He has done rather than what we do, the more we will respond in service from an overflow of love in our lives.

➤ *Why do you think it is difficult to live by grace rather than by rules? How does our performance-based culture increase this challenge?*

takeaway

Grace is God's work from eternity past transforming our eternity future. (It's all about God!)

training points

What are three ways you could serve others as an overflow of God's grace in your life? Write them down below and discuss one way you can serve together as a group to help someone in need.

10. _____

11. _____

12. _____

transforming others

Who will we serve as a group this week by God's grace?

How can I reorient my actions to serve out of an overflow of God in delight rather than from duty?

the coach's perspective

Ask your players, "When a teammate makes a mistake that hurts our team, how should we respond?" (You may be surprised at their answers!) After hearing their thoughts, ask, "How would you want your teammates to respond when you make a mistake on the field?" After their responses, share for a few moments about some specific attitudes we should commit to on and off the field to show God's grace even in the midst of mistakes. You can also end by having each player write a short note of encouragement to another player to close your time together.

> *"These things I have spoken to you while abiding with you. But the Helper, the Holy Spirit, whom the Father will send in My name, He will teach you all things, and bring to your remembrance all that I have said to you."*
>
> —JOHN 14:25-26

YOU'VE GOT GAME 5

(THE ATHLETE AND GOD'S SPIRIT)

Supernatural competition requires supernatural power.

From 1914 to 1988, 5,687 consecutive day games and zero night games had been played at the Chicago Cubs' Wrigley Field. For many years the no-night-games policy was due not to a lack of electricity but rather to a deep sense of tradition surrounding the Cubs' legacy. After long planning and much preparation (along with threats from MLB that Chicago would have to play all of its playoff games in St. Louis!), Wrigley Field finally changed its policy. On August 8, 1988, the Cubs hosted its first-ever night home game. This game against the Philadelphia Phillies was rained out after three and a half innings, but the next night, the Cubs beat the Mets 6–4. Thousands came to watch history being made, sharing in a new era under lights.

Though the Cubs had the potential to play night games for years, it could never happen until someone decided to set up and turn on the lights. The Holy Spirit functions much the same way. All of the power we need to live an abundant life in Christ already exists within us. We just need to turn on the lights.

When God saved us, He gave us everything needed for spiritual growth and victory. God has given us a new mind, new heart, new conscience, and new emotions—all of this through the new covenant put into effect by the death and resurrection of Jesus Christ.

Yet we are limited people. We cannot accomplish all of God's plans for our lives with our own power. Only as we are empowered by the indwelling Holy Spirit will our lives produce God's intended results. *Supernatural competition requires supernatural power.*

The Holy Spirit is God's supernatural gift to help us live as the new people God has created us to become. The Spirit is the heart and soul of a healthy and growing Christian life. If we don't use His power, we will continue to limit our spiritual development. But once we are empowered by the Spirit, we will experience the supernatural capabilities of a life where God's grace flows through the conduit of our new nature, keeping our spiritual lives bright and alive as servants of Christ.

God's Supernatural Signing Bonus

In 2006, the Arizona Cardinals signed former Indianapolis Colts tailback Edgerrin James to a four-year contract worth $30 million, which included a signing bonus of $11.5 million.

We live in a time when professional athletes not only ask for, but often expect, a signing bonus. In some ways, it has ceased to function as the special gift it was intended to be.

This is also how we as believers can find ourselves treating the Holy Spirit. Sometimes we need to be reminded that the Holy Spirit is God's great gift to us. In John 7:37–39, Jesus stood on the crowded streets of Jerusalem and declared that those who believed in Him would experience living water springing from their innermost being.

> the Holy Spirit's job is to run interference so we can move forward in our spiritual lives.

In verse 39 John says, "This He spoke of the Spirit, whom those who believed in Him were to receive; for the Spirit was not yet given, because Jesus was not yet glorified." Something that is given is a gift, which is exactly what the Bible calls the Holy Spirit.

Unfortunately, many believers today function as if the Holy Spirit is the bench player of the Trinity. They know He is there, but they don't let Him in the game very often. Yet the Holy Spirit is the most active member of the Godhead when it comes to spiritual growth, so it's vital we learn what God's Word says about Him.

1. What the Spirit provides

As a fullback, one of my (Jonathan's) primary tasks is to run interference for the halfback, opening up holes for him to get through. It is my job to enable the running back to make forward progress down the field. Likewise, the Holy Spirit's job is to run interference so the believer can move forward in his or her spiritual life.

As believers living after Christ's resurrection and the birth of the church, we are accustomed to Jesus' physical absence and the Holy Spirit's invisible presence. It is what we have always known. This was not the case with His disciples. When Jesus announced His imminent departure and the Holy Spirit's coming in the Upper Room, it created a significant crisis.

During the team meeting that night, Jesus announced, "Where I am going, you cannot come" (John 13:33). His disciples were in a panic. They had been with Jesus for three years and looked to Him for everything. How were they going to function without their Leader?

Jesus knew His disciples were upset, so He answered their questions with this promise: "I will ask the Father, and He will give you another Helper, that He may be with you forever" (John 14:16).

This verse contains two key words. The word "another" in the Greek language means another of the same kind. God was not sending His people a cheap stunt double or a future round draft pick, but Someone just like Himself—a Person with the same essence and character as Christ. The Holy Spirit is God, the third person of the Trinity, sharing the same essence and power as Jesus.

The other key word in John 14:16 is "helper," a word that means one who is called alongside to assist. A few verses later Jesus said, "The Helper, the Holy Spirit, whom the Father will send in My name, He will teach you all things, and bring to your remembrance all that I said to you" (verse 26).

Jesus' promise of the Holy Spirit's coming was fulfilled on the Day of Pentecost (Acts 2), when the Spirit came to indwell the followers of Christ and empower them to accomplish Christ's work. This promise is now made real to each believer at the moment of our salvation, when the Bible says we are baptized by the Spirit into Christ's body (1 Corinthians 12:13).

It's important to distinguish here that this baptism is not some special emotional experience we have to seek *after* conversion, but something that happens *at* conversion. In basketball you don't get an assist after the play, but right when the shot is made. Paul made this especially clear by saying, "If anyone does not have the Spirit of Christ, he does not belong to Him" (Romans 8:9).

If you know Christ personally, the Holy Spirit lives within you at this very moment. According to Jesus, the Spirit wants to flow through you and out from you to others as a rushing river of blessing and refreshment. In John 7:37–38, Jesus said, "If anyone is thirsty, let him come to Me and drink. He who believes in Me, as the Scripture said, 'From his innermost being will flow rivers of living water.'"

➤ *What are some ways you have experienced the Holy Spirit working in your life? How can you tell the difference between God's Spirit working in you and your own human efforts?*

2. What the Holy Spirit does not provide

While the Holy Spirit serves as an incredible gift, few function under the full extent of His power. Too often we try to live life in our own strength. It's similar to an athlete who keeps going on his own, refusing to quit playing even after he has been handicapped by a serious injury.

This persistent determination to be strong on one's own might be admired on the athletic field, but it doesn't work when it comes to the Holy Spirit. In the end, it results in more harm than good. If you had all the power you needed on your own, you wouldn't need the Spirit. His energy would not be necessary. But Jesus said, "Apart from Me you can do nothing" (John 15:5). When Christ transformed us, He gave us Someone to lean on who has the strength to heal our wounds. He gave us the Holy Spirit because He knows that supernatural issues must be encountered with supernatural power, and there is no power greater than the Holy Spirit.

The Holy Spirit will never help self-sufficiency. He will only respond to our dependency. Many Christians are like high jumpers who propel themselves eight feet in the air to get over the bar. God gave us the Holy Spirit so we could become pole-vaulters going nineteen feet. The difference between a high jumper and a pole-vaulter is dependence. The former is dependent on human power, the latter upon the leverage of leaning on something else to take them higher.

If you're tired of the results you've gained from trying to live a good life in your own strength, your problem may be that you're using the wrong power source. The Holy Spirit lives in every believer, but not every believer allows Him full control of their lives. This comes through the Spirit's filling, which opens up the rivers of living water that He wants to send flowing through us.

➤ *Why do we try to live life by our own strength rather than God's strength? When do you find it easiest to turn over control to God's Spirit in your life?*

Is It *in* You?

A series of Gatorade commercials offered the penetrating question, "Is it *in* you?" While Gatorade is referring to its line of sports drinks, the question can convict us in our spiritual lives. The Bible makes it very clear that even though every Christian possesses the Holy Spirit, it is possible to experience very little of His power and influence in our daily lives. *The issue is not how much of the Spirit we have, but how much He has of us.* Ephesians 5:14–17 tells us it is possible to be a Christian, yet also to be asleep and weak spiritually.

1. What it means to be filled

Paul begins with the words, "Do not get drunk with wine, for that is dissipation, but be filled with the Spirit" (Ephesians 5:18). What happens when people drink too much alcohol? They lose control. Paul's idea is that the opposite of being out of control is to be filled with the Holy Spirit.

When you are filled in the New Testament sense, it means that somebody or something else has taken control of your life and is calling the shots. You are no longer in charge but rather a player obeying the calls of the Coach.

This command is in a form in the original language that means "keep on being filled." It's a continual process. You don't resist Satan once and are then done with him for the rest of your life. The Spirit's filling in our lives must be constantly and continuously renewed each day.

> ➤ *Why do you think so many people misunderstand the concept of being filled by the Spirit? How does it look in your life to be filled by the Holy Spirit?*

2. Why it helps to be filled

Scuba divers have a tank of air attached to them that connects them with the real world while they live in a foreign one. The tank is their life source while they are immersed in water. The Holy Spirit is the believer's life source for living a godly life in the foreign environment of this world.

When God's Spirit controls your life, your life begins to look more Christlike. No longer do the addictions of alcohol, drugs, pornography, lust, or any other vice hold control over us when the Spirit is in control. A life empowered by Him takes our spiritual duty and makes it a spiritual delight.

Living for Christ is not a matter of trying but a matter of dying. When we give up our life to be consumed by God's Spirit, we discover results that are far greater than those we could ever produce on our own. Not only can we win, but we can blow out our spiritual opponent, Satan, because our power through the Spirit is much greater than his.

Red Bull Faith

In recent years, several new energy drinks have begun appearing on the shelves of grocers, in health stores, and gyms. One of the most popular of these is call Red Bull. Consisting mostly of water and caffeine, the drink is popular with college students during exam week, among young people at dance parties, and with truck drivers needing energy for the road.

The Holy Spirit is the Red Bull of our faith. Without it, we tire and grow weary early in the battle. With it, God gives us the strength to accomplish supernatural service for His glory. How does a person experience the Red Bull effects of God's Spirit? Ephesians 5:19–21 touches on the issue:

> Speaking to one another in psalms and hymns and spiritual songs, singing and making melody with your heart to the Lord; always giving thanks for all things in the name of our Lord Jesus Christ to God, even the Father; and be subject to one another in the fear of Christ.

These words address the means to being Spirit-filled rather than the results of being filled. Paul's concern here is to tell us how to be filled and stay that way. The Holy Spirit's filling is made real when we make worship our lifestyle.

1. Off-season worship

You can always tell who is committed to off-season training and who is not. Those who did not come to training camp or preseason find themselves panting between plays, frequently stopping for breaks, and displaying less of an edge than their teammates.

Jerry Rice, the great NFL receiver, provided a picture of off-season training at its finest. Part of his off-season workout schedule during his years with the 49ers was a two-and-a-half-mile uphill park trail in San Carlos, California. His normal routine was to train each day from 7:00 a.m. to noon. Cornerback Kevin Smith described it by saying, "What a lot of guys don't understand about Jerry is that with him, football's a twelve-month thing."

Has it worked? His statistics speak for themselves: first in the NFL for most career receiving yards, career touchdowns, career receiving touchdowns, career receptions, and season receiving yards, plus ten consecutive Pro Bowl appearances. Jerry Rice is considered by most players as the greatest receiver to have ever played in the NFL.

Many of us treat Monday through Saturday like the player who neglects training in the off-season but expects to make the highlight reel at game time. Sunday worship gatherings are designed to maximize our conditioning from the rest of the week, not to build us up to last until next week. What would you say if a hockey player was interviewed after a game and said, "I think that game really prepared us for the off-season. We should come back much stronger next year from the lessons we learned on the ice"? You'd probably ask, "Are you kidding me? The off-season is the time to train, not game day." You would be exactly right. Game day is the time to reflect all of your training in a way that makes the greatest impact for your team.

The same is true of us as believers. How we prepare during the week shows during our times of worship with other believers. It's like the old boxing saying: Champions don't become champions in the ring—they are merely recognized there. Worship is what we do every day to display our love for God and honor Him. Such worship involves finding God's viewpoint in matters from His Word, deciding to live in light of His will and dependence on the Holy Spirit for the power to pull off the decision to obey God's Word. Paul calls this having the mind set on the Spirit (Romans 8:5–7).

➤ *Share about your off-season sports training routine. Why do you train the way you do? How could this same discipline be used by God's Spirit to help in your spiritual training?*

2. Game day worship

There is nothing quite like game day in college football. It begins with tailgate parties, bands, fans, and an air of unparalleled excitement. Players arrive hours before kickoff to mentally and physically prepare for the brief window of action about to begin.

While our worship is an everyday pursuit, gathering with other Christians for worship can be very similar to a college football game day. In a church where God's Word is proclaimed and His praises sung, there is a sense of anticipation that touches everyone present. Such environments also allow you to feed from the energy of others, keeping you from giving up and throwing in the towel.

In the early church, God was at work in this way. Acts 2:43 tells us, "Everyone kept feeling a sense of awe." Why? Because God was at work in a group of people devoted to Him on a daily basis (Acts 2:46). This first community of Christ-followers was experiencing God at work so powerfully that we find "the Lord was adding to their number day by day those who were being saved" (2:47).

➤ *How would your church be different if every person was as committed to being filled with the Spirit each weekday as they were on Sunday? What could you do personally to help make this more of a reality in your life?*

Staying On Track

Let's shift direction as we talk about the Holy Spirit as the enabler of our spiritual growth. In Galatians 5:16–17, Paul writes, "But I say, walk by the Spirit, and you will not carry out the desire of the flesh. For the flesh sets its desire against the Spirit, and the Spirit against the flesh; for these are in opposition to one another, so that you may not do the things that you please."

The issue in Ephesians 5 is who will be in control. The issue in Galatians 5 is who will conquer. One way you know you are a Christian is that you feel a battle warring within you between your sinful desires and the Holy Spirit's righteous desires. The Bible tells us repeatedly that God and human desires will never get along because they are directly opposed to each other. Just as an offense and defense are dramatically opposed to one another with no possibility of cooperation, even so the flesh and the Spirit can never work in harmony in the believer's life. That's the whole point Paul made in Romans 6–8 when he finally cried out, "Wretched man that I am! Who will set me free from the body of this death?" (Romans 7:24). His answer was that victory is found in being "in Christ Jesus" (Romans 8:1). That's where the Holy Spirit wants to keep us.

Paul challenges us to walk by the Spirit so we won't live for this life's wrong desires. It's easy to misread Galatians 5:16 as saying, "Walk by the Spirit and you will not have the desires of the flesh." As much as we might wish this were true, history proves quite the opposite. It's often those who seek God most fully whom Satan chooses to attack most fiercely.

1. Walking by the Spirit is a daily process

Former heavyweight fighter Joe Frazier once said, "You can map out a fight plan or a life plan. But when the action starts, you're down to your reflexes. That's where your roadwork shows. If you cheated on that in the dark of the morning, you're getting found out now under the bright lights."

The concept of walking by the Holy Spirit is similar to being filled with the Spirit, but the image of walking makes it easier to picture the ongoing aspect of the Spirit's work. Walking is something we do every day. In fact, we walk so often that we often miss that it consists of three distinct but critical parts.

First, walking involves a destination. When you walk, you're going some-where, even if it's just across a room. Walking by the Spirit involves a destination, too, because He is always moving us toward a destination—God's glory. Jesus described the Holy Spirit's destination when He said of the Spirit, "He will glorify Me" (John 16:14). When you walk by the Spirit, you're going somewhere.

Second, walking requires dedication. Most people don't just take a few steps and then quit for the day. Anyone who does that won't get very far, because walking must continue if we are to make progress. It's like the Holy Spirit's filling, which must be renewed regularly. It must be ongoing. As NBA Hall of Famer Jerry West observed, "You can't get too much done in life if you only work on the days when you feel good."

Third, walking includes dependence. You have to put your weight down on one leg and then on the other to walk. If your legs aren't working properly, you have to depend on additional assistance to get you where you're going. Either way demands dependence.

When I (Tony) broke my leg playing football in high school, the ambulance came onto the field, paramedics picked me up, and they took me to the hospital. I was immediately taken into surgery and had a steel plate inserted in my leg. The doctor gave me crutches to walk with because I was too weak to stand on my own.

Pride will keep you from leaning on the Holy Spirit, too. Pride says, "I can do it myself." Now if I had tried to walk out of the hospital after surgery on my broken leg, I would have fallen on my face and discovered my great weakness. Sometimes God has to let us fall on our face before we will look to Him and say, "I get it, God. I'm ready to lean on Your Spirit and walk Your way." When you come to the place of recognizing your dependence, you are ready to learn what it means to walk by the Spirit. When you begin regularly calling on the Holy Spirit to empower your obedience to God, you will experience personally the power of His work in your life.

➤ *Why do you think it is so difficult to walk by God's Spirit on a daily basis? What could we do to make the process easier?*

2. Walking by the Spirit fuels growth

We all know what happens when a baby in his mother's womb decides it's time to get out—there is no stopping him! The mother and the rest of the world have to adjust to the baby, not the other way around.

That's what happens in the spiritual realm when we learn to walk by the Spirit. It's no accident that Galatians 5:16–17 talks about walking by the Spirit and is then followed by verses 22–23 that describe the fruit of the Spirit. Once we discover how to walk in God's power, we can begin to produce a life that displays His power. The result is that our lives overflow with an abundance of fruit that can be enjoyed by those around us.

With spiritual growth there is no limit on how fast you can grow or how far you can go. The Holy Spirit will take you as far and as fast as you are willing to depend on Him and give up trying to live by your own strength. The proof that we are growing will be that our actions and attitudes, character, and conduct will increasingly reflect the character of Christ.

➤ *What relationship do you see between walking in the Spirit and living out the fruit of God's Spirit? How have you seen this take place in your life?*

takeaway

God's weakest link is stronger than our greatest strength. (Remember, apart from Christ we can do nothing.)

training points

What steps could you take this week to better live a life filled by the Holy Spirit? How can you help each other in your group in this process?

13. _____

14. _____

15. _____

transforming others

Who would be the first people to notice radical changes in my spiritual life? How will I explain the difference to them of being filled with God's Spirit?

Who are a couple of people I can pray for this week as I seek to walk by the Spirit even in my prayer times?

the coach's perspective

Ask your players, "Can you name some ways we depend on each other as teammates?" They will likely respond with the different roles they play, such as blocking, playing goalie, or dribbling, depending on the sport. Then ask, "How do we depend on God's Spirit as a team?" You may hear silence. If so, use this teachable moment to share that even more important than depending on any teammate, we are designed to depend on God's Spirit to enable us to perform at our best. If time permits, take a look at Samson's dependence on God's Spirit in Judges 15:14–17.

GOD'S PLAYBOOK

(THE ATHLETE AND SCRIPTURE)

Knowing the play determines whether you make the play.

P eyton Manning's approach to football has completely changed the way teams play in the NFL. Traditionally, an offensive coach calls in a play, the quarterback shares that play in the huddle, and then the team runs that play. Not so with Peyton Manning and the Indianapolis Colts. Instead, offensive coach Tom Moore calls in what he calls "concepts," allowing Peyton to call the best play at the line based on what defensive structure his opponent prepares. He will often change the play up to three different times before taking a snap, keeping both his team and his opponents on high alert.

While such an offense has greatly improved the Colts' win record in recent years, there is one major problem for his teammates. With so many play changes, sometimes a wide receiver or lineman will either not hear the latest change or not remember which play was called last. As a result, you will occasionally experience a play in which a Colts receiver runs in the opposite direction of the passing route, or where a lineman is given a penalty for run blocking during a pass play. In the end, the saying is true: *Knowing the play determines whether you make the play.*

For followers of Christ, our plays are the truths found in God's Word. Our play-book is the Bible. Jesus Christ directly addressed the connection between spiritual growth and Scripture when He said, "Man shall not live on bread alone, but on every word that proceeds out of the mouth of God" (Matthew 4:4). Far too many Christian athletes today know their team's playbook much better than God's playbook. Spiritually speaking, you are unable to make the play when you don't know the play the Coach is calling.

Mere reading or memorization is not enough when dealing with the Bible, just as memorizing an offensive play is not enough to execute it. When learning the Scriptures starts to become just another course for our transcript, we can find ourselves increasing in Bible knowledge while struggling to live for God spiritually. Jesus told some of the spiritual leaders He confronted that their study didn't help because it did not lead them to believe in Christ (John 5:39–40).

First, we must be absolutely clear that the Bible is the inspired, perfect Word of God (2 Timothy 3:16; Matthew 5:17–18; Isaiah 55:8–9). It is not just a book to give us information, but a playbook for life that must be understood and acted upon for our spiritual benefit. It is the specific tool the Holy Spirit uses to make us like Christ.

➤ *What different views do people have about the Bible? How does this affect the way we talk about the Bible with other people?*

The Proper Diet

For athletes, the proper diet is critical in preparation. The sale of energy bars alone generates over $100 million a year. When discussing the importance of God's Word in our lives, then, the apostle Peter chooses a diet-specific theme to relate: "Like newborn babies, long for the pure milk of the word, so that by it you may grow in respect to salvation" (1 Peter 2:2).

What milk is to a baby's diet, the Word of God is to the soul. It is the food that fuels healthy spiritual development. Peter shows that we are not talking about an occasional snack on God's Word. A baby pursues milk with a passion that will not rest until her hunger is satisfied. It doesn't matter to a baby whether it is 3:00 p.m. or 3:00 a.m. When a baby is ready to eat, nothing else matters.

1. A select diet

Peter referred to the Word as "pure" milk. He gives the idea of uncontaminated, 100 percent all natural, with no substitutes added. When an athlete pursues a particular diet, he checks labels to make certain the ingredients he needs are the ingredients used. Carbs, fats, proteins, calories, vitamins—all are recorded in great detail. Nothing less is acceptable.

Some athletes forget to show as much discernment regarding their spiritual diets. Too often a mere snack is expected to satisfy. Mediocre church attendance or an occasional glance at a few verses of the Bible **many believers have let themselves get out of shape spiritually.** cannot serve as the select diet necessary to develop a healthy spiritual life.

Even worse, some find spiritual substitutes that are the equivalent of a juice that advertises itself as having "10 percent real fruit juice." There may be some truth to it, but such a substitute cannot replace authentic Christian growth. As Christians, we must seek a select diet of pure milk from God's Word, not accepting any substitutes.

➤ *What substitutes do you see people using in place of God's Word for their spiritual growth? How do these substitutes fail to satisfy?*

2. A scheduled diet

Other followers of Christ are not benefiting from the Word the way they should because they are not passionate for the Word on a regular basis. They have forgotten the importance of a regularly scheduled diet for their spiritual health.

Diligent athletes cannot just diet for an hour on Sunday morning and expect to be in top shape for competition. Why do we try to get by doing it spiritually? Using Peter's analogy, babies eat regularly for the simple reason that they are hungry. Why don't we feed on God's Word more than we do? The answer is simple: we don't hunger for it. Our approach should reflect the words of Job, who wrote, "I have treasured the words of His mouth more than my necessary food" (Job 23:12).

Believers who don't live with a scheduled diet of God's Word will fail to stay competitive spiritually. Church attendance cannot replace a regular, daily diet of truth that flows from a passion and hunger for God.

➤ *What do you think would be the perfect diet of Bible reading for your daily life? What would have to change in order for this to happen?*

3. A specific diet

One question we've not yet discussed is, "What exactly is the milk of the Word?" The milk of the Word stands for the basics of the Christian faith. This specific diet is described in Hebrews 5.

The readers of the letter to the Hebrews had been Christians for a long enough time that they should have been teaching other people, but they still needed to learn again "the elementary principles of the oracles of God" (Hebrews 5:12). Verse 13 calls these basic principles "milk."

Of course we all need to know these essential truths. After all, we don't see a person who has never played baseball signing a multimillion-dollar contract with the Yankees! There is a progression of learning the basics, excelling over time, and developing into a professional.

You'll never see a NASCAR driver jump out of his car shouting, "Look, now I know how to drive!" It's good to know how to drive (especially if you're in NASCAR!), but for someone who has been an athlete for years, to be content with knowing the basics such as how to shoot a free throw or swing a bat is not enough. This progression is what the Bible calls the "meat" or "solid food" of the Word. It is being able to use the truths of Scripture to address the issues of life on a consistent basis.

➤ *What were some of the first skills you had to learn in your sport? What would your performance look like if you were still struggling in these basic areas?*

The Right Training

As an athlete, you know that a proper diet alone is not enough. Without training, the best foods are of little value. There must be hours of weight training, sprints, distance running, skill development, and drills. These will vary depending on the sport, but the common trait of training for victory is required for success for anyone.

1.   Athletes who don't train

We've all seen it. The athlete who has made it to some level of success has now decided to stop training to stay at the top. What happens? The person gets out of shape, loses focus, and eventually falls from the status once achieved. Likewise, many believers have let themselves get out of shape spiritually by not training themselves beyond the basic beliefs of the faith.

Peter addressed his plea to baby Christians, those who were new enough believers that their spiritual digestive systems were too young to handle solid food. There's nothing wrong with a two-month-old infant feeding on milk. But when you see a twenty-year-old with a bottle hanging out of his mouth, you can be sure something is wrong!

In Hebrews 5, the readers are accused of such immaturity: "Concerning him [Melchizedek] we have much to say, and it is hard to explain, since you have become dull of hearing" (verse 11). They had not trained diligently in God's truth and were now struggling as a result.

The church in Corinth is another example of believers who had not trained hard to develop in their faith. Paul had to tell them, "And I, brethren, could not speak to you as to spiritual men, but as to men of flesh, as to infants in Christ. I gave you milk to drink, not solid food; for you were not yet able to receive it. Indeed, even now you are not yet able" (1 Corinthians 3:1–2). The accusation is clear; they had not trained hard and were not ready to run God's plays.

➤ *Share about a game or competition where you felt unprepared. What made you feel that way? How can these same feelings of being unprepared hurt us spiritually?*

2. Athletes who train hard

Former NBA player Scottie Pippen became an all-star player during his years with the Chicago Bulls. However, many would be surprised to find out that he did not even win a starting position on his high school basketball team until his senior year. At the University of Central Arkansas, he started out as the team manager. His play quickly improved, though, and by his senior year he was the starting guard and the best player on the team. He eventually was selected for seven all-star games, played on two gold medal–winning Olympic teams, was instrumental in the Chicago Bulls' six NBA championships, was a three-time All-NBA First Team, was an eight-time All-Defensive First Team, was the 1994 All-Star MVP, and was named one of the NBA's top fifty players of all time.

Scottie's story offers several spiritual parallels to what we encounter in Hebrews. Hebrews 5:14 makes this crucial statement: "Solid food is for the mature, who because of practice have their senses trained to discern good and evil." Mature believers have the ability to choose right and wrong because of the training they have from knowing and applying God's Word. The more consistently you connect truth with life application through the trials and challenges God allows to come your way, the more mature you become in your relationship with God.

➤ *Think of a skill you've learned in your sport that directly impacts how you play your game now. How does continued practice of this skill pay off in your performances?*

3. The difference it makes

The New England Patriots' Tom Brady had quickly become one of the best-known quarterbacks in the NFL. Brady shocked the football world in 2002 during what was only his second season by becoming the youngest quarterback to win the Super Bowl, defeating the St. Louis Rams 20–17, and becoming the second youngest to earn the Super Bowl MVP. He eventually led his team to three Super Bowl victories in eight years. What makes him so good? A recent *Sports Illustrated* article mentioned that of all his talents, perhaps his most valuable ability was being able to translate skills from the practice field into real-time game situations.

The last half of Hebrews 5:14 provides the key to knowing when we have transitioned from the practice field to the game field, properly trained to live out God's plays. The answer is not just when we have the drills and skills. A well-trained athlete has developed to maturity when he or she can implement the skills in specific game-time situations that help the team win.

As believers, we must feed on the milk of God's Word, but we must also move on to learn the meat of the Bible as well. The goal is to know God's plays so we can run God's plays. It is not enough to *know* the right answers—we must also be able to *live* as the right answer.

This was the hope the writer of Hebrews shared with his readers: "Therefore leaving the elementary teaching about the Christ, let us press on to maturity" (6:1). Hebrews also shows us why God's truth can provide such maturity: "The word of God is living and active and sharper than any two-edged sword, and piercing as far as the division of soul and spirit, of both joints and marrow, and able to judge the thoughts and intentions of the heart" (Hebrews 4:12).

A two-edged sword cuts on both sides, which means it cuts coming and going. To explain it another way:

- ■ *The Word of God* is so sharp that it can pierce the deepest parts of our being.
- ■ *The soul* is our personality, the part of us that makes us who we are.
- ■ *Our spirit* refers to the new nature that God placed in us.

The Word can sort things out in our lives even when there is so much noise we can barely hear the play. In other words, the Holy Spirit can use the Bible to help separate the stuff you can't separate. If you are ready to train passionately in God's truth, you'll find all the strength you will ever need.

➤ *How can you tell the difference between an athlete who is well-trained for your sport and one who is not? Looking at your spiritual life, what are some areas that need more training spiritually?*

The Difference in the Pros

If you've ever talked with someone who has played football both in college and in the NFL, you'll hear a common story. In college there are *some* hard hitters, but in the NFL *everyone* hits hard. *Every* play is performed at a more intense level. Spiritually, this is very similar to the difference between the believer who is content with the milk of the Christian faith versus the person who craves the meat of God's Word. For the mature, *every* play is performed at a higher level. The difference is between those merely familiar with the truth and those who know it and use it in everyday applications.

1. The relationships are different

When high school basketball phenomenon LeBron James made the jump directly to the NBA, an interviewer asked him what differences he noticed among the players with the Cleveland Cavaliers from those in his high school. He answered that his top area of struggle was regarding relationships. In his high school, his friends talked about things like who they would take to prom. In the NBA, his teammates were talking about what their own kids were doing in school. Big difference!

It was the same sport but different people. The people you spend time with indicate a lot about you. Jesus had many people around Him who were called His followers at one point or another. Large crowds also followed Him, but He knew that most of them were following for the wrong reasons, so He only taught them in large groups rather than spending a lot of time with them individually.

On one occasion Jesus sent out seventy of His followers (see Luke 10:1), but He was not as close to them as He was to the twelve apostles. Even in this group He drew closest to Peter, James, and John. From these three men, much of our faith has been influenced. Peter was the early leader of the church and writer of two Bible books. James became the first apostle to die for Christ, setting an example that countless others would follow. John cared for Mary the mother of Jesus, wrote five books of the New Testament, and is the apostle who lived the longest, influencing the second generation of Christians perhaps more than any other apostle.

Why were they so influential? A big reason is because they were so close to Jesus. When it comes to knowing God's Word, the ultimate reason is to grow closer to the Ultimate Author, Jesus, whose words we seek to know and follow.

> *How does knowing the person involved in a story change how we listen to the story? How can viewing the Bible as Christ speaking to us change how we read Scripture?*

2. The expectations are different

When a college football player is drafted into the NFL, everything changes. The practice level increases, the hours of film footage multiply, and the off-season training routine turns into a full-time job. The expectations of a mature believer are much higher as well. The Bible says one mark of growing and maturing Christians is their ability to teach others (Hebrews 5:12). You know you are making progress in your spiritual journey when you not only learn the Word for yourself but find yourself communicating what you learn with others.

Spiritual maturity requires that you read God's Word so you . . .

- know what it says (Revelation 1:3),
- know what it means (2 Timothy 2:15),
- meditate on it for application (Psalm 119:11),
- listen to it being taught (Hebrews 5:13–14), and
- transfer its truths to others (Hebrews 5:12).

But if you will drink the pure milk of God's perfect Word and graduate to its solid food, you will discover that it's good for you. You will grow in grace and the knowledge of our Lord Jesus Christ. Then you will be able to say with Jeremiah, "Your words were found and I ate them, and Your words became for me a joy and the delight of my heart; for I have been called by Your name, O Lord God of hosts" (15:16).

Study God's playbook so you can run the plays well during the game of life. Remember, you must know the play to make the play.

➤ *Of the five areas of Bible growth mentioned above, which area is your strongest? Your weakest? What has been one of the most helpful ways you have found to learn Scripture?*

takeaway

You must know the play to make the play. (Knowing God's Word is not automatic!)

training points

What new steps do you want to pursue to better know God's Word? Write them below and share them with your learning group.

16. _____

17. _____

18. _____

transforming others

Who in my group can I share with about my Bible reading this week?

What is one thing I can do this week to share something from God's Word with someone who may not be living for Christ?

the coach's perspective

Ask your players, "How well would we play as a team without someone calling each play?" You may even want to show this in action, allowing those in your group to run a couple of plays with no direction. After hearing their answers, respond with the reminder that the Bible is our playbook as Christians. Without playing from a common source, we would be moving in different directions that hurt us as a team. Discuss some ways you can grow together in God's Word as a team, possibly memorizing a key verse together such as 1 Timothy 4:12 or Joshua 1:9.

"Therefore let us draw near with confidence to the throne of grace, so that we may receive mercy and find grace to help in time of need."

—HEBREWS 4:16

WHAT PLAY DID HE CALL?

(THE ATHLETE AND PRAYER)

Communication is critical to success in athletics and in life.
It's critical in your spiritual journey, too.

T he most overlooked person on the baseball field is the third base coach. Most fans don't even notice him. Even those on his own team do not pay attention to him most of the time—unless they are on first base.

Once on first base, the base runner must closely watch the third base coach's every signal. Do I steal second base? Has a bunt been called? A sacrifice fly? If the next batter hits the ball to advance the runner, that runner must keep his head up to know if he is being waved to run home or whether to stop safely on the next base.

How well the base runner pays attention to his coach greatly determines how well he advances. Ignoring his coach's signals could cause him to be thrown out, hurting his entire team in the process.

Communication is critical to success as an athlete. It's critical in your spiritual journey, too.

Prayer can simply be defined as relational communication with God. Prayer is not just a ritual of words that we must say in the right order or a task to mark from our daily list. Jesus clearly rejects this external, performance-based understanding of prayer (Matthew 6:5–7). Prayer is part of a relationship with God to be cultivated.

We often use a lot of flowery words when we start talking about prayer, but for many people prayer has little to do with the realities of life. Consider how many people think of prayer:

- Some people think of prayer like the national anthem at a ball game: a nice opening ritual that has nothing to do with what happens on the field.
- Other people treat prayer as a good-luck charm, a spare tire, or a rabbit's foot to pull out and rub when things are tough.
- Still others treat prayer as a Christmas list, asking for all of their wants with little regard for a relationship with the One to whom they are praying.

It's possible even for followers of Christ to approach prayer in such superficial ways. Yet God has made us in such a way that the power of the Holy Spirit rides along the waves of prayer, making prayer absolutely vital and central to all of life—including our spiritual growth. Prayer is so important that the Bible tells us, "Pray without ceasing" (1 Thessalonians 5:17).

When football teams play at Invesco Field at Mile High Stadium, the Broncos' home stadium in Denver, you will often see players wearing an oxygen mask on the sidelines. Literally a mile high in altitude, the stadium provides the ultimate home-field advantage against those not acclimated to such conditions. We could illustrate the centrality of prayer for the Christian by substituting the word *breathe* for *pray* in the verse above: "Breathe without ceasing."

We don't breathe only when we feel like it. We don't say, "I don't feel like breathing today," and stop breathing. We don't get frustrated with breathing and say, "This isn't getting me anywhere. I'm not going to do this anymore." We must breathe! We draw from the breath in our bodies as if it were life, because breathing is essential to functioning in this world. God wants prayer to be *that* essential in our lives.

The Ultimate Home-Field Advantage

Paul tells us in Ephesians 1:3 that we live "in the heavenly places in Christ." In addition, we are seated with Christ in those same heavenly places (Ephesians 2:6).

Heaven is where our Father lives, and prayer is how we communicate with Him. The goal in prayer is to enter our Father's presence the way a child comes to a loving father.

Prayer as relational communication with God is a wonderful concept. Yet even the most devoted Christian can sometimes feel as if on a foreign field that looks far different from where he is used to playing.

1. We are playing on a different field

When you play a game at a different location, you can feel uncomfortable and a little lost because it looks and feels so different from what you are used to at home. The colors, the locker rooms, even the words and language used by the local fans often stand out as unfamiliar. The language of the heavenly playing field is prayer, and since the heavenly playing field is the source of our power, victory, peace, joy, and everything else we need to grow, it is essential we learn to understand the language of prayer.

The good news is that we have the perfect Coach for the job, the Holy Spirit Himself. One of the Spirit's roles is to teach us the language of prayer and to guide us in learning how to pray. The Bible says the Holy Spirit can even translate our prayers to God when we don't know what to say.

Paul writes, "We do not know how to pray as we should, but the Spirit Himself intercedes for us with groanings too deep for words" (Romans 8:26). The Holy Spirit understands prayers that we can't adequately express. He makes sense of thoughts that we don't even personally understand, because He knows the language of prayer and can interpret it to us.

We need to pray without ceasing because prayer is the link between the physical and spiritual playing fields. The Holy Spirit will communicate God's heart back to us by connecting with our human spirit so we will hear God talk with us in the deepest part of our being. This is why prayer cannot be run like a hurry-up offense. Extended prayer allows the Holy Spirit to share God's thoughts with us so we begin thinking God's own thoughts in our minds (1 Corinthians 2:12–13).

▶ *Why are you glad that the Holy Spirit intercedes for us before God's throne? At what times do you especially need His intercession?*

2. **It's like game day**

When no opponent is in your home stadium, the advantage of the home field is unseen. But its true power is experienced on game day. On game day, fans seem to come in a blur as they arrive in your team's colors, sing your team's songs, cheer your team's cheers, know your team's stories, and share your team's emotions. From cheerleaders and fans to signs and music, the experience changes the environment.

That's what the Holy Spirit wants to do for us. The link in the process is prayer. When we pray, we are transported to an experience that is completely different from our everyday world. Game day is short and temporary, but prayer is much different. Prayer transports us to the spiritual realm, where Jesus is sitting at the right hand of God and we are seated with Him. Prayer positions us to hear from God, so our new spiritual life is ready to be spoken to by the Holy Spirit. Then we are ready to hear God applying His Word to our specific needs and circumstances.

The Devil doesn't want you to understand the power of prayer. This throws his entire game plan off course. Satan can't keep you from praying, but he attempts to make you feel weak, frustrated, and powerless in prayer so you will give up more easily.

Let's face it. Real prayer is hard work. We may have good intentions as we bow to our knees, but we can fall asleep, run out of things to say, or find our minds wandering after just a few minutes. Like a pulling guard, prayer allows eternity to interfere with history when we are willing to merge our will into God's will, but it must change us internally as well. Focused conversation with our heavenly Father redirects our understanding of the world around us. Prayer helps turn us from a self-focus to a Savior-focus so we can accomplish His will.

➤ *Share about a game day when you felt a huge adrenaline rush because of the experiences surrounding the event. How is this similar to what God desires for us during our times of intimate prayer?*

3. Our head coach has provided a game plan

Jesus had a lot to say about prayer during His short ministry on earth. During His Sermon on the Mount, He outlined an incredible game plan for prayer. Jesus said:

> When you pray, you are not to be like the hypocrites; for they love to stand and pray in the synagogues and on the street corners so that they may be seen by men. Truly I say to you, they have their reward in full. But you, when you pray, go into your inner room, close your door and pray to your Father who is in secret, and your Father who sees what is done in secret will reward you. And when you are praying, do not use meaningless repetition as the Gentiles do, for they suppose that they will be heard for their many words. (Matthew 6:5–7)

These brief statements rocked the common perception of prayer in Jesus' day. Challenging the idea that prayer was a public demonstration for entertainment, He made it clear that it was not a matter of saying all the right words in the right order. The intimate nature of our communication

we don't have to feel that God is beyond our reach.

with God is illustrated by going into a closet and closing the door behind us to pray. Why shut the door? Because it's just you and your Father in a private conversation.

This was not a ruling against public prayer. The kind of prayer Jesus condemned was the kind done to impress other people and gain their favor. This same twisted view of prayer is evident in people who box it into a ritual of certain words spoken in a certain order. While many of us may think we're okay because we don't read prayers from a book, we can still fall into our own patterns of rote prayer. When some people say they don't know how to pray, what they really mean is they don't know how to pray the way they hear other people pray. They think they don't know all of the right words to speak in public.

Jesus said you don't need to worry about getting all the words right because "your Father knows what you need before you ask Him" (Matthew 6:8). God still wants you to ask, but He is more concerned about your worshiping than your wording. He isn't grading us on how well we express ourselves. He just wants us to come to Him as a child to a loving father who desires to be a part of every aspect of his child's life.

> *Where do you go for your personal times of prayer? Do you have a "prayer closet" area of your own? If not, where would be a good place to begin such a prayer habit? How do you feel when asked to pray in public? Why do you feel that way?*

Our Coach Has Played the Game

When choosing a new coach for a team, those deciding usually desire a leader who has played before at the same level. For instance, if choosing a new Division I baseball coach, a college would prefer a leader who had played Division I baseball or professionally. Why? Because that person can lead from personal experience.

The same is true of Christ. Hebrews 4:14-16 emphasizes this truth:

Since we have a great high priest who has passed through the heavens, Jesus the Son of God, let us hold fast our confession. For we do not have a high priest who cannot sympathize with our weaknesses, but One who has been tempted in all things as we are, yet without sin. Therefore let us draw near with confidence to the throne of grace, so that we may receive mercy and find grace to help in time of need.

These verses reveal four great lessons that can turn anyone's prayer life from dormant to dynamic. They help because our Coach, Jesus Christ, has played in our position before us.

1. His person—He is on our team

The writer of Hebrews tells us right up front that the most important fact about our High Priest is His identity. He is on our team. "Jesus the Son of God" is a great title for our Lord, indicating both His humanness and His sacredness. Jesus is unique in eternity and in history because He is the God-man. As man, He can feel what we feel. As God, He can fix our feelings as well.

Job said, "For He [God] is not a man as I am that I may answer Him, that we may go to court together. There is no umpire between us, who may lay his hand upon us both" (Job 9:32–33). Job was looking for someone who would take his hand and identify with him. Yet he also needed someone who could take God's hand and identify with Him, bringing the two of them together.

We don't have to feel that God is beyond our reach because Jesus has bridged the gap. He can understand what you are going through when you cry out to Him, and He has the power to do something about it. A priest represents the people to God and God to the people. We have a High Priest who understands both sides perfectly, just like a coach who has played for our same team in our same position before us. Jesus is unique in His Person.

➤ *Have you ever felt that God was out of reach? What difference does it make in your life knowing that Christ has removed this gap?*

2. His position—He has all access

A photographer must have an all-access pass to stand with the team on the sidelines and take pictures during the game. While anyone can take pictures from the stands, a person with an all-access pass stands in a unique position.

Jesus is also unique in His position. He has "passed through the heavens" (Hebrews 4:14). Once a year in Old Testament times, Israel's high priest would go behind the curtain into the Holy of Holies to atone for Israel's sins. There were many priests, but only the high priest could perform this act.

What you want to do in prayer is go to where God's throne is. The problem is that you and I can't get there without some help. Why? Because no one has ever gone from earth all the way there—except Jesus, who has passed through earth to heaven and is now praying for us in the very temple and throne room of God.

When we pray in the power of the Holy Spirit, Jesus makes sure our prayers reach the proper location where our needs and concerns can be addressed. As God's Son, He has direct access to the Father and communicates our needs directly to Him.

> ➤ *How can knowing we have access to God through Christ strengthen our prayers? What does this truth have to do with the tradition of ending our prayers with praying in Jesus' name?*

3. His passion—He sympathizes with us

A third aspect is Christ's passion, His feelings of sympathy for us. Jesus knows how it feels to play through injury and to be penalized unjustly. He can relate to us, sharing these feelings with God the Father.

God the Father already knows everything actual and potential. His knowledge is complete. However, the Father has never been tempted to sin in the way we are tempted. He knows all there is to know about sin, but He has never experienced the temptation to sin like Jesus has.

God the Father wanted to relate to us on an emotional level. He sent His Son in a human body with emotions like ours so His Son could feel everything we feel. No matter what temptation you face, Jesus knows what you are feeling because He experienced it at one time. When you pour out your heart to God, Jesus acts as your Great High Priest before His Father, saying, "Father, I know what this person is feeling. I know what it is like to be under their pressure. I sympathize with Your child in need of Our help." He sees the tears and the struggle.

> ➤ *How does Jesus' sharing in our human emotions help you when you pray?*

4. His provision—He wants us to win

Hebrews 4:16 says we can "draw near with confidence to the throne of grace, so that we may receive mercy and find grace to help in time of need." We don't have to hold anything back in prayer. We don't have to question whether we are wasting our time or if this is doing any good. Like any good coach, Christ wants us to win.

During the 2002 college football season, I (Tony) traveled to see my son Jonathan play for the Baylor University Bears. Jonathan threw for a touchdown and caught a twenty-five-yard pass, so it was a great game. I was scheduled to speak to the Baylor team before the game, and I had two friends with me. They did not have authorization to enter the locker room. Then when we walked through the door, I identified myself and told the security officers the men were with me. Their names were not on the list, but they gained access on my authorization. They walked into the locker room with the same confidence as I had because they were connected with me. My friends were able to move about freely because someone authorized went ahead of them and opened the way.

God says you have been authorized to enter His throne room because of your connection with Christ. It is a throne of grace. It is a throne because the One who sits on it is the Ruler of the universe. As a ruler, He longs for His followers to succeed in their battles.

Our Father gives us what we don't deserve and could never earn from a throne that never runs low on its provision. He desires that we draw near in prayer. God has all the grace we need to help us, but we have to ask for this grace.

How can we have a High Priest like this and not draw near to Him in prayer? When you encounter the power of prayer, you will start to quickly develop, as your new life grows stronger in its proper spiritual environment.

You may say, "But I'm tired."

That's okay. Just draw near.

"But you don't understand. I'm hurting and I feel like quitting."

I may not understand, but Jesus does. Draw near to Him. He will meet you where you are and take you before the throne that dispenses grace. No matter what may be happening in your life, Jesus stands ready to lead you directly into His Father's presence, where there is unlimited grace to meet your needs.

Pay attention to the plays He calls, and experience the amazing relationship of intimate communication with God.

➤ *What challenges do you experience when you're trying to draw near to God? How can you more passionately focus your prayers?*

takeaway

You must look to the Coach to know your play. (Communication is the key in your prayer life.)

training points

What are some new habits you would like to develop in your prayer life? Write them below and discuss them with your group.

19. _____

20. _____

21. _____

transforming others

Using Hebrews 4:16 or another verse on prayer, put a large copy of the verse on the wall in your room, locker, or other place where you will see it daily. When you do, take a moment to pray for someone on your mind who is in need.

Who is one person you specifically need to pray for this week? Commit to daily prayer for this person and specifically share with this person that you are praying for them.

the coach's perspective

Ask your players, "What would happen if we could not hear each other on the field?" Their responses will likely include not knowing the play to run, misunderstanding when to substitute, and similar communication breakdowns. Then share how prayer is the way we communicate with God. If we do not listen to or communicate with Him, communication breakdown occurs and results in spiritual defeat. Spend as much time as possible during this session actually praying, allowing each person to pray out loud to help in the process.

"Let us consider how to stimulate one another to love and good deeds, not forsaking our own assembling together, as is the habit of some, but encouraging one another, and all the more, as you see the day drawing near."

—HEBREWS 10:24–25

HOW'S YOUR BENCH? 8

(THE ATHLETE AND THE CHURCH)

A winning team always has a deep bench of players.

The NBA has long recognized the value of the sixth man by honoring the top bench player with the Sixth Man of the Year Award. In 2005, the Chicago Bulls' Ben Gordon became the first rookie to ever receive this honor. Gordon's play has even earned him the nickname Mr. Fourth Quarter, due to his high-scoring streaks down the stretch, surpassing league leaders Kobe Bryant and Tracy McGrady with the most double-digit games during the fourth quarter. Averaging just over twenty-four minutes of play per game his rookie season coming off the bench, Gordon still averaged 15.1 points per game, providing just the extra strength needed to win many of Chicago's games.

Coaching legend John Wooden won ten college basketball championships and greatly understood the value of strong bench players. He noted, "Unselfishness is a trait I always insisted upon. I believed that every basketball team was a unit, and I didn't separate my players as to starters and subs. I tried to make it clear that every man plays a role."

A winning team always has a deep bench of players.

This is true in the sports arena and in the spiritual arena. God has designed His followers to develop in the context of a community known as the church. The Bible says that our Enemy, the Devil, "prowls around like a roaring lion, seeking someone to devour" (1 Peter 5:8). One of the easiest people to devour is the believer without teammates within the context of the church.

The church is the most exciting team God has placed on this earth. God never meant for us to grow in isolation from other believers. Spiritual growth is a group project.

Adam's aloneness was the only part of creation that God said was "not good" (Genesis 2:18). By giving Eve to Adam, God was stating a fundamental principle—that He created human beings to exist in community.

We do not attend church services just to hum songs and hear sermons. We need to be part of the church because it is the environment God has created for our maximum spiritual growth. Apart from the church, our spiritual growth is stunted.

Some people will tell you they love Christ, but hate church. However, Christianity doesn't work that way. That would be like saying, "I love playing soccer. It's my teammates I can't stand." Jesus Christ is so committed to His church that He died and rose again to redeem us. Our relationship to the church is so vital that there is no such thing as maximum growth without the church. The bold but honest truth is that Christians who refuse to become committed to a local church are living in sin because they are living in disobedience (Hebrews 10:24).

> *What is your church background? How has your church background influenced your thoughts about the benefits of church involvement?*

You Can't Play without a Team

The church is not just a classroom for spiritual instruction, but a living and growing organism to enhance our spiritual journey. It is the team Christ is coaching. Ephesians 2 offers the Bible's clearest words regarding this concept:

> So then you are no longer strangers and aliens, but you are fellow citizens with the saints, and are of God's household, having been built on the foundation of the apostles and prophets, Christ Jesus Himself being the corner stone, in whom the whole building, being fitted together, is growing into a holy temple in the Lord, in whom you also are being built together into a dwelling of God in the Spirit. (verses 19–22)

We are part of something much bigger than ourselves. Paul reveals to us that the family of God we belong to is "growing." There is no mention here of personal growth apart from the church. The pronouns are all plural. We grow as we are connected to our teammates because it is the church huddled together that experiences the unique presence of God (Ephesians 3:10, 17–21).

1. The power of a team

There are some things God will do for you just because you are one of His children. Then there are many other things God will do for you only when you are a committed teammate of His church. Spiritual growth can only reach its fullest potential in your life *through* the church.

It's the difference between watching your favorite college basketball team on television all alone versus watching the game on a giant plasma screen with your best friends. You experience the same game, but there is a certain energy found only when joining together with others for the event. The laughter, the tears, the screams—all of the emotions are intensified when gathered with others.

> **God is more interested in our maturity than in our medals.**

There are times, of course, when we need to spend time alone with God. And when people who are individually consumed by God's Spirit come together for worship, learning, encouragement, and service, the Holy Spirit works in a powerful way far beyond what we experience alone. The Christian life is meant to be lived in community. The church is the dwelling place of the Holy Spirit (Ephesians 2:22).

➤ *Name some things in life that are more enjoyable to experience with a group than alone (such as a movie, a road trip, or going to a game). What makes those experiences better as a group? How is this similar to the benefits of growing together in a church setting?*

2. A coach for the team

One reason we gather as a church is to celebrate Christ's victory. We may have a rough week where we feel like losers, but when we huddle with other Christian teammates, we are reminded we are on the winning team. It's hard to enjoy celebration alone. Jesus Christ is so excited about His victory that He has called together His church to celebrate His victory on the cross. Celebration, like other parts of our spiritual growth, is a group project.

A story is told of an incident in the Special Olympics where the competitors lined up to run the hundred-meter dash as best they could with their limitations. Everyone took off, but one of the runners fell and began to cry. All of the other runners stopped, came back, and helped the fallen runner stand up. Then, with arms joined , the entire group walked across the finish line together.

This is a touching story, but one you would probably never see in the regular Olympics. In fact, during another Olympic game a sports magazine carried the photo of a famous woman runner who had been favored to win the race; instead she was pictured holding her leg in agony after a fall on the track as the other competitors raced past her.

What made the Special Olympics runners turn back and help the person who had fallen while no one stopped during the other race? Those Special Olympians realized that they all had the same weaknesses and shortcomings. They knew it could have been any one of them lying there on the track. In love, they reached out to him, and in a very real sense all the runners won the race that day.

God is more interested in our maturity than in our medals. The talented servants Paul mentions in Ephesians 4:11 are given to the church to equip us for service for "the building up of the body of Christ" (verse 12). This is the power of a deep bench, where Paul ties Christ's victory to the church with the development of His people. Christ desires the church to pursue maturity until all of His people reach Christlikeness (4:15).

➤ *What aspects of the Christian life do you feel are best done together rather than alone? Name some examples from your own life.*

There Is No "I" in Team

A few years ago a young mountain climber in Utah amputated his own arm to free himself after falling among the rocks. One amazing part of the story is that searchers traveled to the area where he had been trapped to see if they could locate the severed arm and bring it back so it could be reattached. Though that attempt failed, it provides a graphic example of how believers in Christ can strive to reconnect severed members to bring wholeness to the body.

As members of the body of Christ, all of us are to stay connected and keep building each other up "until we all attain to the unity of the faith" and to become "a mature man" (Ephesians 4:13). The idea is not to let anyone become disconnected so that it causes damage to the rest of the body.

Many coaches have used the phrase, "There is no 'I' in team." Why is this quote used? It serves as a visual reinforcement that being a teammate requires sacrifice rather than selfishness. In exchange, a team provides two specific spiritual benefits.

1. A team provides passion

The writer of Hebrews had this important word for the church: "Let us consider how to stimulate one another to love and good deeds, not forsaking our own assembling together, as is the habit of some, but encouraging one another; and all the more as you see the day drawing near" (Hebrews 10:24–25). Nothing will provide passion more than joining together with other Christian teammates to worship God, learning and serving together in unity.

We are not to quit gathering as a church because it provides the passion that fuels our spiritual development. As an athlete, when you have a bad game, you need the encouragement of your teammates. The word used for "stimulate" in Hebrews 10:24 literally means to incite or create heat. It's the picture of a fire that burns brighter and longer when many logs are stacked together versus a single log that will burn out quickly. A believer cannot stay hot for God while avoiding God's family.

➤ *What part of church involvement provides the most passion in your life? Why do you think this is the case?*

2. A team provides friends

How would you respond if someone asked you, "Would you like to come to a place where you will be loved, encouraged, and treated as a valuable person?" Most of us would say, "Sign me up!" That's the way the church is supposed to treat its people.

We all long for the part of church that gives to us. However, many people are only concerned about the part that offers personal benefit. When it comes to serving or sacrificing, they run, leaving the body of Christ with a missing body part in the process.

The Bible deals with this problem in 1 Corinthians 12:12–31, speaking again about the body of Christ. After discussing how all the parts of Christ's body need one other, Paul said God's goal was that "there may be no division in the body, but that the members may have the same care for one another" (verse 25). Spiritual growth is a partnership, like two teammates seeking to provide an assist to one another rather than being known as ball hogs.

> *Share about a time when you played or competed in your sport even when you had an injury. How did your injury change the way you played? What parallels do you see that apply to serving within the church as the body of Christ?*

Dream Team Essentials

When Paul described the goal of spiritual growth as maturity, he provided our standard. We should grow "to the measure of the stature which belongs to the fullness of Christ" (Ephesians 4:13).

1. The right standards

If you want to know where our spiritual development leads, look at Jesus Christ. Paul's all-consuming goal was to know Christ (Philippians 3:10). This is a lifelong process. We will never score a perfect 10 until we reach heaven. God simply desires us to pursue Him at full speed.

One way you'll know you are growing is when you increase in spiritual stability. Ephesians 4:14 says, "As a result, we are no longer to be children, tossed here and there." Unstable Christians bounce back and forth from one minute to the next. Stable, maturing Christians can take a hit and keep moving their feet for the next challenge.

To line up in the wrong formation in football is considered a rookie mistake. A coach may look past this in the first practice of the season but would not be as kind if it happened during the playoffs. Likewise, God doesn't expect instant stability from us as Christians, but He does expect us to improve in our pursuit of Him.

> *What spiritual goals do you have in your life? Even if you haven't met your personal goals for your spiritual life, describe what kind of progress you have seen as you have pursued Christ.*

2. The right discipline

For such passionate growth to take place, at least two things need to be present in our lives. Not surprisingly, both are supplied within the church. Instead of being unstable children, Paul says, "We are to grow up in all aspects into Him who is the head, even Christ" (Ephesians 4:15). The elements that produce maturity are found in the phrase at the beginning of this verse: "speaking the truth in love." Truth and love must *both* be present for real growth to occur.

The Holy Spirit's work in the church is essential to growth, but the Holy Spirit only works in the environment of truth. Jesus called the Holy Spirit "the Spirit of truth" (John 14:17). The Spirit's job is to reveal the truth of God's Word and confirm it in our hearts. The church is *the* center for promoting, proclaiming, and protecting God's truth (1 Timothy 3:15).

Truth and love must work in harmony with one another. The church is to be "rooted and grounded in love" (Ephesians 3:17). It's not a choice, but a requirement. It would be like a football team that was all offense but no defense. You may score fifty points per game, but it won't matter if your opponent scores sixty!

Information applied without love can come across as harsh and uncaring. The reverse is also true. If your coach said, "It's okay," every time you made a mistake on the field, you may feel good about yourself, but you would not improve very much. We need to practice confronting those we care about with God's truth, but doing so out of an overflowing love that is clearly shown to the person we confront. This is why we are told to speak the truth in love (Ephesians 4:15).

> *Of the two disciplines, truth and love, which do you find easier to practice? What are some ways you could improve in the area that is more difficult for you?*

3. The right commitment

The last verse in this section of Ephesians 4 really nails down the truth that spiritual growth is not a solo act but is a team effort requiring every part of the body. The verse tells us, "From whom the whole body, being fitted and held together by what every joint supplies, according to the proper working of each individual part, causes the growth of the body for the building up of itself in love" (verse 16).

It's impossible to miss! The body of Christ grows when each and every individual part is functioning properly. The growth of the church is the overflow of the growth of its members. In the same way, the lack of growth by individuals in the church affects the entire body.

In a large baseball stadium there are literally hundreds of lights. If one goes out, not many people will notice. When several lights begin to go out, everyone notices because the teams cannot perform without the proper light. It's the same in the church. Without each of us working together, our team cannot perform well. We can light the way for others only when we are shining together in unity.

Nothing on earth can compare to a group of believers in a local church who are under the control of the Holy Spirit, using their God-given gifts to serve others. When this happens, the entire team builds itself up in love. When believers are growing together in unity and love, a lot of ordinary problems are taken care of before they become big problems, because the body is healing itself. A healthy body that is working the way it was designed to work will grow, and every member of that body will benefit.

When God put together the human body, He did it so that every part would be vital for the working of every other part. The church functions the same way. If you are not in a church where God's Word is being taught in an atmosphere of love, you need to find a place where the body is functioning as God intended. Regardless of whether God's plan for you right now is as a starter or serving from the bench, you need the church for the benefits it brings to you and the benefit you are to the body of Christ.

➤ *What is your church involvement like right now? How would you like to improve the way you are contributing to your local church?*

takeaway

The body of Christ is better together. (A winning team always has a deep bench of players.)

training points

What would you like to change about your local church involvement? Write down a few ideas and share them with your group.

22. _____

23. _____

24. _____

transforming others

Choose one thing you will do to serve someone in your church this week and do it. Be ready to share with your group how God uses this act of service.

Who do you know that you could invite to experience church with you this week? Give them a call and offer to even give them a ride or take them to lunch as part of participating in a worship time together.

the coach's perspective

Ask your players, "How would our games be different if no one came to see us?" The answer would be that they could still play, but the level of excitement would be much different. Then take this discussion a step further, asking, "What if only half of our team showed up for the next game? How well would we do?" Point out that most people think church is similar to showing up to watch a game. It's great to go, but the team can still play fine without them. The biblical truth is that church participation is similar to showing up to play for your team on game day. When you don't show up, the results for you and the team can be disastrous.

PLAYING IN THE CLUTCH

(THE ATHLETE AND PERSEVERANCE)

The best athletes excel when the pressure is greatest.

There are two basic types of basketball players: those who want the ball at the end of the game and those who do not.

Players who excel at the end of the game are called clutch players. Many greats have emerged over the years of NBA basketball, including Magic Johnson, Larry Bird, Reggie Miller, Allen Iverson, and Tim Duncan, but one clutch player has become known as one of the greatest of all clutch players. His name? Michael Jordan.

His statistics alone speak volumes:

- NCAA Division I Champion
- Sporting News College Player of the Year (twice!)
- Two Olympic gold medals
- Six NBA championships
- NBA Rookie of the Year
- Ten-time NBA All-Star
- Highest NBA career scoring average
- Most seasons leading the league in scoring
- Five-time NBA MVP
- Six-time NBA finals MVP

However, beyond his legendary statistics remain stories of legendary last-second shots, clutch free throws, and defining defensive finishes that contributed more than statistics in his team's dynasty of championships.

When the game was on the line, Michael wanted the ball.

The best athletes excel when the pressure is greatest.

Yet unlike those clutch moments in basketball lore, life's trials don't just happen in the last few minutes of a game. They may last for days, weeks, or even years. Even worse, the exact reason for them may never be made clear to us. Life's tests can make us feel powerless. Still, there is one area we can control—how we respond.

To take it one step further, life's problems are actually a vital part of our spiritual development. Problems both reveal our character and test our limits.

Pressure Situations Are Essential for Growth

Many people don't want to hear that struggle is a necessary part of the Christian life, but it's true. The Bible says the hard times we face in life are so important to our growth that we should actually welcome them. Every trial is an opportunity for spiritual development. Hurdlers can't win unless there is an obstacle to overcome. True athletes look forward to the adversity of competition. James puts it this way: "Consider it all joy, my brethren, when you encounter various trials" (James 1:2).

If we are honest with ourselves, we are probably wondering if James can really mean that life's pressure situations can be a joyful experience. It might be a lot easier if he had told us to find joy in life's problems, but he said to consider it *all* joy. This means total joy that is pure and complete. It's the equivalent of telling a basketball player, "You should be excited when you're down by five with under a minute to go." It just doesn't seem to make sense. Fortunately, James provides more of an explanation to his challenge.

1. There will be clutch moments

We would prefer to think of such clutch moments as the exception rather than the norm, but James refers to them as "various trials." This is a unique word in the original text meaning multicolored or multifaceted. You won't get bored by the problems you face because they will come in every color, shape, and size you can imagine. Trials are like the mail we receive at our homes addressed to "Occupant." All you have to do to undergo trials is be alive.

Even worse, James doesn't say "if" you encounter trials, but "when." The word "encounter" in James 1:2 suggests these problems are not of our own making, but are problems from the outside. These are the linebackers causing a fumble rather than the problems we face due to a lack of personal fitness or preparation.

The problems we face come in many styles. Some are circumstances that just aren't going right. We may also encounter physical, financial, relational, or emotional trials that tackle us and disrupt our lives. Whatever the color or shape of our trials, there is nowhere we can go to escape them. Trying to avoid trials is like changing teams hoping to escape the practices. The new team will also require much practice and possibly even more than the team you've just left.

Job said, "Man is born for trouble, as sparks fly upward" (Job 5:7). In Jesus' words, "In the world you have tribulation" (John 16:33). We have a natural tendency to run from trouble, but we cannot run from God's plan. He knows where to find us.

➤ *What do you consider the difference between the problems we create ourselves and a God-ordained problem? How does looking out for the problems God allows to come our way help us to endure them with joy?*

2. Each pressure situation prepares us for the next

Christians obviously aren't the only people who have problems, but there is a great difference between the ones we experience as believers and the troubles of an unbeliever. For the believer, there is no such thing as a problem without a purpose. Every difficulty that comes our way has a reason attached to it. Trials are pain with a purpose, designed to prepare us for the next spiritual battle.

This is because no trial hits your life without passing through the hands of God first. Job's story is a great example. The Devil had to receive God's permission before tormenting him (see Job 1–2). God either sends our trials directly or allows them to come—all as part of His perfect plan.

➤ *Share a recent pressure situation you have endured. How can you see that problem preparing you for something God may have in store for your future?*

Why Do We Have Two-a-Days?

Every August, football teams begin the season with the grueling tradition called two-a-days. As the name indicates, this is the method of piling two full-length practices back-to-back leading up to the first game. It is a time of great preparation and great testing. It's ultimately about endurance. James 1:3–4 says we can rejoice in our trials because we know something important: "Knowing that the testing of your faith produces endurance. And let endurance have its perfect result, so that you may be perfect and complete, lacking in nothing."

1. God desires prepared players

The reason for trials is for our spiritual maturity. The word "perfect" reflects this and is used twice in verse 4 for emphasis. The word means to become mature or to grow up. Spiritual maturity is the process of becoming more like Jesus Christ. It is allowing more of His life to show through our lives. Paul called it "Christ [being] formed in you" (Galatians 4:19).

Now you may be saying, "I don't know. The problem I'm in right now feels like it's destroying me rather than growing me." The idea is not to deny the pain. The statement James makes about the purpose of trials is one we have to take by faith, but it is also a promise from the God whose Word never fails. This has been confirmed by the lives of countless believers who have emerged victorious from various trials over the centuries to show us that God is faithful to bring good even from our hardest times.

The interesting thing about our trials is that they are custom-made. One of the hardest things Paul had to wrestle with was his "thorn in the flesh"

(2 Corinthians 12:7). He called it both a messenger from Satan and something sent from God, a very interesting contrast. Have you ever felt like something in your life was being influenced both by God and the Devil? You may have been more right than you realized.

Why did God custom-make this affliction that apparently was very painful for Paul? He says it was "to keep me from exalting myself" (verse 7) because of the incredible vision he was given of heaven (verses 2–4). Paul's response? "For when I am weak, then I am strong" (verse 10).

God knew what Paul needed, just as He knows what we need. You say you want the power of God in your life? Then expect problems. Expect persecution. Be a prepared player, faithfully and joyfully enduring the obstacles along the journey.

> *What can you actually do to prepare for trials? After identifying some options, consider what preparations will best help in equipping you for God's upcoming battles.*

2. God discovers who is ready

For many years, fans thrilled to Hank Williams Jr.'s musical cry, "Are you ready for some football?" Yes, millions of viewers were ready for Monday Night Football. Fans and players alike talk up who will win and how they will crush the opposing team. But in the end, what is remembered is who shows up and shuts down the other team.

Likewise, it's one thing to talk about God's ability to carry you through any trial. It's another thing to run down the field on the opening kickoff and make it happen. James says that trials are "the testing of your

if you're dropping out of the race before it ends, you'll have to face the same race again and again.

faith" (James 1:3). Trials call your faith to center ring, where it is time to put on the gloves and prepare to fight.

In the days and weeks leading up to the war in Iraq, a typical comment was heard when our troops were interviewed by the media. The line went something like this: "Well, we know we have the best training and equipment available, but we really won't know what we can do until we're in the battle." That's the best reason you can receive as to why God allows us to encounter trials. You will never know what you can do spiritually until you experience the pressure of the battle.

➤ *What is a trial or problem you are going through right now? What "battle" do you need to endure well?*

3. God demands strong finishers

The testing of our faith produces endurance, according to James 1:3. Endurance is the ability to hang in there until the problem is over. But this also means we can't quit halfway through the test. The problem with quitting on an exam is that you will just have to go back and face it again if you want to keep going. Some of us have been seated at the same desk, spiritually speaking, taking the same test for years, because we keep quitting before the test is over. In the words of James, we are not letting endurance have its perfect work so we can become mature.

If you are dropping out of the race before it ends, you will have to face the same race again and again. When we quit in the middle of a problem that is designed for our growth, it delays our advancement. Imagine an Olympic runner pulling up in the middle of the 200-meter dash saying, "This is a hard run. There's no way I can win this one. I'm just going to stop now. Maybe they'll give me another chance." They may give him another chance, but he'll have to wait four years for it!

Remember that God has His hand on the process and knows when to end a trial because its work is complete. In the meantime, He gives us great promises, among them His comforting presence during the trial (Isaiah 43:2–5); the assurance that though we may be "afflicted" or "perplexed" we will not be crushed or in despair (2 Corinthians 4:8); and the promise that no matter what difficulty comes to us, it cannot separate us from the love of God in Christ (Romans 8:37–39).

➤ *What is the hardest practice or game you have had to finish? What made it so difficult to complete? How did that experience help you in the future?*

What It Takes to Excel under Pressure

Now if God allows trials for us to grow, how can we endure these painful times to experience the blessing of spiritual maturity? In James 1:2–12, we find four factors that help us handle trials the way God wants.

1. It takes attitude

First, remember the command in James 1:2: "Consider it all joy . . . when you encounter various trials." James doesn't say that trials are joyful things in themselves, but that we can be joyful in them because God is at work. It has been said that if you really want to do something, you'll find a way; if you don't, you'll find an excuse.

It is also clear that the joy James mentions is not based on how we feel. Happiness is based on what happens, but joy has to do with our attitude regardless of what is happening around us. The joy we can experience during trials is the joy that comes from God and is based on the truth of His Word when we recognize that God indeed has a purpose behind the pain.

➤ *What is your current attitude toward life's problems? How would you like your attitude to be different?*

2. It takes a reality check

Remember James 1:3: "Knowing that the testing of your faith produces endurance." To have joy in our trials, we need to have the knowledge that God is using them for His good. The Devil doesn't want you to know that God can use your times of testing to build your endurance leading to the development that both God and you desire.

Could you imagine Seattle Seahawk running back Shaun Alexander walking up to a referee during a game to say, "Those linebackers are hitting me too hard. Could you just tell them to let me through for the rest of the game?" Of course not! Running backs know that in order to gain yardage, many hits and much pain will be necessary. And Shaun should know, leading the NFL in 2005 with 1,880 rushing yards.

Our greatest example of patient endurance in trials is Christ Himself. Hebrews 12:2 says of Jesus, "Who for the joy set before Him *endured* the cross" (italics added). Joy and death on a cross are two concepts that don't go together in our human minds. But Jesus was able to look past the pain of the cross because He knew that glory awaited Him when He returned to His Father and redeemed His people.

But make no mistake—Jesus still felt the agony of His trial. He prayed just the night before His painful death, "My Father, if it is possible, let this cup pass from Me" (Matthew 26:39). The Bible also tells us He kept His eyes fixed on the outcome of the cross. Jesus knew that God was going to use the horrific pain of Friday to create the glorious resurrection of Sunday.

➤ *How does knowing trials will come in our lives help to better handle them when they do come?*

3. It takes wisdom

It says in James 1:5: "But if any of you lacks wisdom, let him ask of God, who gives to all generously and without reproach, and it will be given to him." God is the source of the wisdom we need during our times of pain.

A word of warning here—this is not an invitation for us to quiz God about the reasons behind every problem. We may not always know why problems come. Instead of asking *why*, we need to ask God *how*, as in, "Dear Lord, how do You want this trial in my life to help me grow spiritually?" This is the kind of question God will honor.

But it's not enough to ask the right questions. We also need to ask with the right motives. According to James 1:6–8, it is possible to ask God for wisdom and then question whether we intend to obey Him or not. James calls this being "double-minded," and he is very clear about the result: "That man ought not to expect that he will receive anything from the Lord, being a double-minded man, unstable in all his ways" (verses 7–8). When you ask God for wisdom, your response needs to be, "Speak, [Lord], for Your servant is listening" (1 Samuel 3:10).

> *In what area of life right now do you desire God's wisdom? Consider stopping for a moment as a group to pray for wisdom for one another's situations.*

4. It takes experience

The reason we need wisdom from God to handle our trials is to keep us from wasting these experiences. When you look at your trials from a human perspective, you'll react humanly by getting bitter instead of better. When we view trials from God's perspective, we can learn valuable lessons that will strengthen our relationship with Him and prepare us for future battles. Nothing is a waste of time if you use the experience wisely.

> *What are some of the most important lessons you have learned from past trials?*

Looking Back at Clutch Moments

When learning a new play in football, often an example is drawn on a play chart showing how it should look. James gives us a play chart for our response to life's problems in James 1:9–11. This play involves two players, one poor and one rich, which connects with us regardless of which side of the financial spectrum we fit or anywhere in between. When viewing our clutch moments, James wants us to learn two important lessons.

1. Keep the right attitude

The old adage goes, "Those who do not learn from history are doomed to repeat it." In other words, if we don't learn from our past problems, we are likely to face them again. The first person James gives us is the poor man, or the person of "humble circumstances," who is told to "glory in his high position" (verse 9). Today this person may be the college student who has to work every spare moment just to stay in college, the laid-off factory worker, or the single mother with three mouths to feed. There doesn't seem to be any answer financially. In these situations it is easy for a believer to become angry at God because of his or her financial situation.

Why would James tell a person in this situation to rejoice? What is this high position? Perhaps God allowed the money to get tight because He wants us to focus on our riches in Christ, which *is* a high position. If this scene describes you right now, don't take your frustration out on God. Let your trial draw you closer to Him as you learn to take your eyes off the physical and focus on the spiritual.

> *Think about a major loss you have experienced in your sport. How did you learn from it to help in future competition? How is this similar to the lessons we learn from spiritual failures in our lives?*

2. Always depend on God

We've all seen the team that has won so many times that they think they are unbeatable. Their attitude becomes proud, their talk boastful, and their actions unmerciful—until they lose. Every streak has its end. Another important lesson as an athlete and as a believer is to stay humble in your victories, acknowledging that all things come from God.

What about those who have the financial means to keep from stressing out? "The rich man is to glory in his humiliation, because like flowering grass he will pass away. For the sun rises with a scorching wind and withers the grass; and its flower falls off and the beauty of its appearance is destroyed; so too the rich man in the midst of his pursuits will fade away" (James 1:10–11).

To be clear, "rich" here is considered anyone who is not "poor." Even if you are not a multimillionaire, consider yourself rich for the moment if you have all of your needs met. If "rich" describes you, it could be that you've never really had to trust God because you've always relied on Visa. The problem with Visa is that you could have your identity stolen, lose your card, or lose your means of financing, and suddenly find your riches fading away. God wants you to understand that riches are like a fading flower that is beautiful today and gone tomorrow.

Both the poor and the rich need to learn that God, and not anyone or anything else, is the source of their security. The poor can rejoice that they are rich in Christ, and the rich can rejoice that they have learned not to trust in their investments. When these lessons are learned, spiritual growth takes place.

➤ *In what ways does money influence our relationship with God? How have you experienced this in your life, either with not enough or with a lot of money?*

What the Clutch Player Wins

In the 1996 Olympics in Atlanta, Kerri Strug faced the trial of her life. She had injured her ankle on the vault and was in great pain as she approached her final attempt to determine whether the U.S. gymnastics team would win the gold medal. She moved the crowd with an incredible performance in spite of the pain she was enduring, and the United States won gold. When asked how she did it, she said she focused on her coach, who kept telling her she could do it and who reminded her of what was at stake. When we are hurting during a trial, we need to put our focus on the right place.

The payoff for being a faithful clutch player is found in James 1:12: "Blessed is a man who perseveres under trial; for once he has been approved, he will receive the crown of life which the Lord has promised to those who love Him."

A little-known fact about Michael Jordan is that in addition to his numerous buzzer beaters, he also missed over three hundred last-second shots during his career. It takes a lot of pain and frustration to become a great clutch player. Yet over time your perseverance will bring great victory, a crown of life as a reward you can enjoy today and for eternity.

takeaway

Pain precedes perseverance. (Remember, the best athletes excel under the greatest pressure.)

training points

List a couple of your recent or current struggles. What are some lessons God may be teaching you that will be important in your future development?

25. _____

26. _____

27. _____

transforming others

Who do I know that is struggling right now that I can encourage?

What will I do this week to encourage them with the love of Christ?

the coach's perspective

Ask your players, "What happens when we play a great game but then stop putting in our best effort during the last few minutes of the game?" The answer will be that they lose the game or at least allow the competition to significantly gain on them. The same is true in the Christian's life. You might play well most of the time, but if you stop putting in your best effort, your results will not be what you want. To excel in your walk with God, you must persevere during the most difficult moments in your life.

End this time by asking what difficult life issues your players have that you can pray about together as a team. Also use this opportunity to provide other practical assistance for requests that might be needed.

"God is faithful, who will not allow you to be tempted beyond what you are able."

—1 CORINTHIANS 10:13

STAND YOUR GROUND

10

(THE ATHLETE AND TEMPTATION)

The best offense is a great defense.

February 2006 marked the entry of a fresh class of athletes into the NFL's Hall of Fame in Canton, Ohio. Among the picks was the late Reggie White, a thirteen-time Pro Bowl selection and former Super Bowl champion with the Green Bay Packers. At six feet five inches and three hundred pounds, he intimidated quarterbacks during his fifteen-year career with 198 sacks and over 1,100 total tackles.

While much was made of Brett Favre and the Packers' offense during the late 1990s, one of the strongest stories was of the ability of the Packers to limit the scoring opportunities of opponents. As one coach put it, *the best offense is a great defense.*

The same is true when it comes to the issue of temptation in our lives. Our best fight consists of a strong defense against the various shapes, sizes, colors, and forms of temptation in our lives. It is part of the spiritual battle we must fight if we are going to move forward in the grace and knowledge of Jesus Christ.

Welcome to Temptationville

God's Word stands clear about the nature of temptation and how it functions. James, for instance, addresses temptation this way: "Let no one say when he is tempted, 'I am being tempted by God'; for God cannot be tempted by evil, and He Himself does not tempt anyone. But each one is tempted when he is carried away and enticed by his own lust" (James 1:13–14).

These verses come immediately after a discussion about persevering through life's problems and trials. This connection is important, because the same Greek root word translated "trials" in James 1:2 is used in the verb form for "tempted" in verse 13. The difference is that a trial (or life problem) is allowed by God to strengthen us in faith; a temptation is an enticement to rebel that comes from the Devil and his demons. It's an invitation to disobey God and results in limited spiritual growth. To put it another way, a trial is designed to develop you; a temptation is designed to defeat you.

God doesn't test our faith by setting us up.

1. Satan wants to defeat you

We must understand that Satan can turn a trial into a temptation to defeat us and drag us down. This has been the case since the garden of Eden, when God put a tree in the midst of the garden and told Adam and Eve, "From the tree of the knowledge of good and evil you shall not eat, for in the day that you eat from it you will surely die" (Genesis 2:17). This command was a trial to test their desire to obey God.

Then Satan turned that trial into an opportunity for evil. He tempted Eve with a desire to be like God, claiming that God was not telling her the whole story. God designed the trial, but Satan twisted it into a temptation. There are many other examples we could discuss from everyday life. A financial issue in your life could be from God to help you depend on Him. If you have turned to excessive gambling to attempt to pay for your financial hardships, you have allowed Satan to turn your trial into a temptation.

Sometimes the differences between trials and temptations are very different. There is no way that a temptation to sin sexually can be something sent from God. He doesn't test our faith by setting us up. Just because you can access pornography for free on your computer doesn't mean God must think it's fine to view it. That's the kind of rationalization Christians sometimes use, even unconsciously, but it just doesn't work. Temptation is different from trials in its origin, its objectives, and its outcome. Temptation is a work of the Enemy from start to finish.

> *Share a recent area where you sensed an unusual degree of temptation. In what ways were you tempted to rationalize the behavior to make it feel acceptable to do?*

2. God wants you to win

James promised that God does not tempt us. God wants you to win against temptation. He is absolutely holy and separate from sin. Jesus said, "The ruler of the world is coming, and he has nothing in Me" (John 14:30). There is nothing in God that can respond to evil, so He cannot be the source of bringing evil to you or anyone else. God is the source of everything good in our lives (James 1:17).

God won't cause you to sin—and the Devil can't make you sin, either. He can offer you a temptation and make it inviting, but he cannot force you to sin. You have to cooperate. The Devil's power is influence and deception, not coercion.

> *Why does it feel like you cannot resist temptation sometimes? What would be the biblical response to this challenge?*

The Stages of Temptation

James 1:14–15 are two verses to commit to memory because they clearly outline the process that temptation takes from a seemingly innocent start toward deadly consequences.

Stage 1: Desire

Stage one begins when a person is "carried away and enticed by his own lust" (verse 14). The word "lust" indicates a strong desire. There are legitimate desires that can turn to illegitimate ends when they dominate your thinking and life. You can eat to live or you can live to eat. One nourishes the body; the other causes an unhealthy lifestyle.

Satan excels in taking God's good gifts and mixing them with deception and empty promises to entice us. It's important to realize that almost every temptation to sin emerges from an honest, God-given desire. If a temptation did not contain some positive desire, it would not be a temptation for us. The allure of temptation in the words of the original language to describe a fisherman putting a worm on a hook and throwing it into the water to entice a fish to bite. The fish is looking for its own lunch, not looking to become lunch for the fisherman. No mouse intentionally looks for dinner in a mousetrap.

Many of us are in debt because of deception. We desired to buy something because of how it made us look or feel, regardless of whether we had the money budgeted to buy it. Through a high-interest credit card or bouncing a check card purchase, a purchase of only a few dollars can easily cost double its original cost.

➤ *In what areas have you been "carried away and enticed" by legitimate desires that cause trouble when misused?*

Stage 2: Disobedience

The second stage downward in temptation is taken when this desire leads us to disobedience. "Then when lust has conceived, it gives birth to sin" (James 1:15). According to this verse, sin doesn't take place until the temptation is accepted and acted upon. It's good news to know that it's not a sin to be tempted.

Hebrews 4:15 says that Jesus was "tempted in all things as we are, yet without sin." So don't stress out over temptation. The only people who are never tempted are those in a cemetery. Our response to temptation determines whether it becomes sin. Jesus talked about someone who "looks at a woman with lust for her" as committing sin (Matthew 5:28). This is looking, and then looking again with the specific purpose for personal pleasure. At this point the will is engaged and the look becomes sinful. It's a deliberate decision of the mind.

> *How easily can you tell the difference between desire and disobedience? What are some practices you have used to stop desire before it turns to disobedience?*

Stage 3: Death

James tells us there is one final stage in the progress of temptation—death. "When sin is accomplished, it brings forth death" (1:15). Sin never stops until it brings about death—either eternal death for the unsaved or a disconnect in the believer's closeness with God, the essence of death.

Of course, we don't physically die every time we sin, but a death does occur. God told Adam and Eve they would die the day they ate of the forbidden tree, and they did. Their fellowship with God shattered. Spiritual and physical death entered humanity. Christians who yield to temptation lose fellowship with God and stunt spiritual growth. This is why the confession of sin remains so important.

The Devil conveniently promotes false advertising to entice us to sin. Sin doesn't come with a label that reads, "Warning: Will Cause Death." Sin appears attractive on its surface. The price seems reasonable. It's a rare person who can stretch beyond "the passing pleasures of sin" (Hebrews 11:25) in favor of obeying God.

Sin will take you further than you want to go and cost you more than you want to spend. It's a roller-coaster ride that ends with a crash. Nothing stunts growth faster than death, and nothing stunts spiritual growth faster than allowing temptation to bring death.

> *What is a habit in your life right now that is stunting your spiritual growth? How does realizing this habit lead to loss of closeness with God affect you?*

Sources of Temptation

Sin's damage can quickly send us to the injured reserve list. Since injury (and death!) serves as the greatest fear of an athlete, it's vital to discover the source of this temptation and resist it with God's power.

Let's use an example from current events. Al-Qaeda, headed by Osama bin Laden, uses terrorism as a tactic to inflict destruction. Waging war on terrorism is not as clear-cut as waging war in a conventional sense. The use of terror reveals how pervasive and difficult tracking down evil can be. It involves a multitude of people operating with stealth and deception. This terrorist triad—an evil leader, an evil system, and evil desires—resembles the often-unseen forces at work against us spiritually. The biblical terms for this triad are the Devil, the world, and the flesh.

1. The Devil—an evil leader

The Devil is the head of this team that tempts Christians to sin. Though he has lost the battle for our eternal souls, he can cause great damage in our lives when we allow him to. Matthew 4:3 even names Satan "the tempter" when he tempts Jesus. If God will allow His own Son to be tempted by Satan, we should also expect He will allow us to be tempted as well. Satan has been provided access to fight this world at this time.

Satan works best by attacking our thoughts. Approaching Eve in the form of a serpent, Satan gave her the idea of eating the fruit God had forbidden in the garden. He promised she could be like God. Eve wasn't standing there trying to figure out how she could disobey God. Satan provided the thought for her.

As believers, we must realize that the initial thought to do something wrong does not come from us. God's new nature within us would not create a sinful thought because it is perfect. The origin of sinful thinking is the Devil. When we listen to these Devil-prompted thoughts, we sin because of the continuing battle with our human will.

Satan studies us the way a football coach studies game film of his opponents. The Devil knows your tendencies and weak spots. He knows what temptation would have the best chance of success against you. The Devil is not all-knowing or all-powerful, but he can influence and plant thoughts and hit us where we are weakest.

Despite his influence, we are promised, "No temptation has overtaken you but such as is common to man; and God is faithful, who will not allow you to be tempted beyond what you are able, but with the temptation will provide the way of escape also, so that you will be able to endure it" (1 Corinthians 10:13). God will not allow temptation beyond your capacity to overcome. You might feel like you can't handle it, but God can still provide strength for your time of weakness.

Satan cannot force you into a corner where you cannot escape. He can throw together an attractive-looking deal like he did with Jesus during His temptation (Matthew 4:1–11), yet notice the flaws in the offerings Satan provided. First, Satan promised Jesus *satisfaction*. Jesus was hungry, so Satan tempted Him to turn stones into bread. This satisfaction left out God, the One Jesus knew was His source of complete satisfaction.

Second, Satan tempted Jesus with *success*, but a personal success without God. He led Jesus to the top of the temple, urging Him to jump off. God will protect You, and everyone will believe You are the Messiah. In other words, Satan was suggesting that Jesus could accomplish His mission without dying on the cross. He was tempting Jesus with the easy button. Again, Jesus knew He had to endure the cross to fully please His Father.

Finally, Satan promised Jesus *significance* without God by offering Him the leadership of the world if Jesus would just bow down to him. Jesus saw through Satan's evil plan and countered him with Scripture, affirming that God alone is worthy of worship.

That's quite a deal Satan provides, because our desires for satisfaction, success, and significance are God-given. The difference is that Satan wants us to pursue these values without God. As the tempter, Satan continues to lead his evil franchise.

> *Of the three areas Satan used to tempt Jesus (satisfaction, success, significance), which one do you find most difficult to stand against? How can studying Christ's response help in overcoming this area in your life?*

2. The world—an evil life perspective

Our second enemy is the world, Satan's evil life perspective that he promotes at every opportunity. First John 2:15 tells us, "Do not love the world nor the things in the world. If anyone loves the world, the love of the Father is not in him." The Greek word for "world" is *cosmos*, the root of our English word "cosmetic." The word means to arrange or put in order, similar to what takes place when women apply cosmetics to prepare for the day.

In this verse, the reference to the world doesn't simply mean planet Earth, but the world's way of thinking. When we talk about the world of politics or finance, we are not speaking of the physical world but a certain sphere of thought. While we live in this world, we don't have to love its wrong ways.

Sometimes what the world offers us appears attractive, making us feel like losers if we do not participate. Don't listen to this world's false advertising! It's like offering you a free autograph of your favorite athlete without telling you that you will have to stand in line three hours in the cold to get it. As the apostle John said, "The whole world lies in the power of the evil one" (1 John 5:19).

> ➤ *Christians tend to live in one of three responses to the world—isolation, integration, or infiltration. We can either run from the world, join the world, or live our faith in the world. Which of these three is the most biblical approach? How can you put your answer into practice?*

3. The flesh—our evil lusts

Our third enemy is our own flesh, our human will that gives the world and the Devil an entry point into our lives. Romans 7:18 reminds us "nothing good dwells" in our flesh. Paul's frustration over doing wrong even when he wanted to do right reflects the battle every one of us must face. Fortunately, in addition to identifying the problem, Paul also gave us a formula for victory over the flesh: "Walk by the Spirit, and you will not carry out the desire of the flesh" (Galatians 5:16).

The desires of our flesh won't go away. We will carry them throughout our lives. The Devil, the world, and the flesh are constantly calling us, trying to draw us away from God. That's the bad news. The good news is that we have the power to defeat these powerful foes regardless of their strength.

➤ *What does it mean to walk by the Spirit rather than by the flesh? How does doing so look in your life?*

Putting On Your Uniform

As powerful as our enemies appear, they do not compare to our God's power. First John 4:4 boldly challenges us that "you are from God, little children, and have overcome them; because greater is He who is in you than he who is in the world." James 4:7 puts it this way: "Resist the devil and he will flee from you." Sometimes we may feel defenseless, but the Bible reveals three critical parts of our spiritual clothing to help us overcome our evil opponents.

1. Attitude: suiting up our thought lives

The spiritual uniform we need is found in Ephesians 6: "Be strong in the Lord and in the strength of His might. Put on the full armor of God, so that you will be able to stand firm against the schemes of the devil" (verses 10–11). Our strength is in the Lord and His might, not in the limited power of our human will.

The reason we need God's strength is that our battle "is not against flesh and blood, but against the rulers, against the powers, against the world forces of this darkness, against the spiritual forces of wickedness in the heavenly places" (verse 12). Our battle is supernatural, and we need the supernatural armor of God to emerge victorious.

When we dress ourselves in God's armor, all we have to do is "stand firm" (verses 11, 13–14). Why does the Bible tell us to stand firm instead of "go fight"? Because in Christ the battle is already won. We're not fighting *for* victory, but *from* victory. Jesus won the battle over the world, the flesh, and the Devil.

➤ *Who is our spiritual battle really against? Not against? How does this influence how we treat those who do not know Christ?*

2. Armor: suiting up for game time

No football player would play a game without a helmet, shoulder pads, and other essential padding because he knows that they are the only source of protection from the opposition. Without the proper protection in a rough game like football, it is inevitable that someone will get hurt. Notice the importance Paul provides regarding each portion of the spiritual armor in Ephesians 6:14–17.

The first piece is the belt of truth. "Stand firm therefore, having girded your loins with truth" (verse 14). I was once flying with a friend who explained to me how important it is to trust the airplane's instruments no matter what your senses tell you, because you can easily become disoriented in flight. Your eyes may tell you you're right side up when you are actually upside down and heading for disaster. God's Word is our instrument panel, and we have to believe it no matter what our senses or the Devil may be telling us. The Bible says, "Let God be found true, though every man be found a liar" (Romans 3:4).

The second piece of God's armor is the breastplate of righteousness (Ephesians 6:14). The breastplate covers your heart. When you know God's truth, your heart knows how to beat at the right rhythm. When you let go of truth, God sets off a warning alarm inside that something is wrong—and it's not wise to ignore warning signals from your heart.

Recently I (Tony) set off the metal detector at the airport, so I emptied my pockets and walked through again. The alarm sounded again. The guard said, "Sir, you must have metal on you somewhere. We're going to have to check you." He checked me with the wand and found nothing. Then he waved the wand toward my shoes, which had a piece of metal in the bottom. In the end, the detector didn't lie.

When God sets off an alarm in your heart, when your spiritual pulse becomes irregular, He's found something you may not see or even know is there. The Holy Spirit connects God's truth with your heart so you deal with sin. The breastplate of righteousness keeps Satan from penetrating your heart with his lies.

The third section of the believer's armor is the shoes of peace (verse 15). The connection to shoes suggests the need to stand firm. The shoes of a Roman soldier gave him sure footing as he fought on unsteady ground. You don't want to trip and fall during battle. Shoes also indicate you are going somewhere. God tells us to stand firm, not stand still. There is nothing static about the spiritual life. Spiritual growth requires constant movement and development, and God confirms our direction by giving us an internal sense of well-being.

The shield of faith is the fourth piece of armor and the first we are told to take up. This shield allows us "to extinguish all the flaming arrows of the evil one" (verse 16). Satan's arrows, spiritual weapons such as doubt and discouragement, are designed to distract us from the real battle. Faith enables us to snuff out those arrows.

If you're under attack, you are also going to need the helmet of salvation (verse 17). A helmet protects your mind, including the new identity you have in Christ. Your salvation is not just fire insurance from hell, but includes everything you are in Christ—a completely forgiven, redeemed, empowered child of God.

The final piece of armor is the sword of the Spirit, "which is the word of God" (verse 17). It's important to note that the word for Scripture here is not *logos*, but *rhema*, which means "to speak." This word refers to our use of God's Word to defeat Satan in battle, using Scripture to confront the specific problem at hand.

The best example of the *rhema* of God in action is the way Jesus answered Satan in the wilderness. During all three temptations, Jesus answered, "It is written" (Matthew 4:4, 7, 10). The Devil can counter your human responses, but he has no answer for the Word of God.

Think about it—if Jesus, the living Word of God, used the written Word of God to deal with Satan, how much more do we need to use the Word? We learn the Bible to live it. When Satan strikes at us with temptation, we can answer him with the Word. The sword Paul referred to here is not a *Braveheart*-sized broadsword, but a short sword used for close-in fighting. When Satan closes in, thrust the Word at him.

> *What one piece of our spiritual armor is an offensive weapon? How should this influence our focus on Scripture?*

3. Appeal: suiting up with prayer

We should be glad Paul didn't stop with just the armor, because one key to the effectiveness of a soldier's armor was putting it on correctly so the pieces fit together to provide maximum protection. Ephesians 6:18 encourages us, "With all prayer and petition pray at all times in the Spirit, and with this in view, be on the alert with all perseverance and petition for all the saints."

How do we put on the armor of God? Prayer. Praying in the power of the Spirit clothes us for spiritual battle. A great exercise is to pray specifically at the start of every day, asking God to clothe you with each piece of His armor for the battles ahead. Begin each morning preparing physically and spiritually for the day ahead.

> *How many words are used to refer to prayer in Ephesians 6:18? How is each of these words significant?*

takeaway

Temptation is an opponent we can defeat through Christ. (Remember, the best offense is a great defense!)

training points

What major temptations have you faced recently? Share some of these with your group and discuss how you can use God's armor to overcome each one.

28. _____

29. _____

30. _____

transforming others

What temptation do I struggle with that I can use to help others with similar experiences? Who is one person I can begin trying to help this week?

Who can I pray for this week regarding a particular area of temptation? Take a moment during your week to write a note or e-mail of encouragement regarding your prayers for them this week.

the coach's perspective

Ask your players, "What areas of practice are you tempted to cheat on the most?" This will vary by sport, with answers such as skipping warm-up exercises or not running the full distance during a required sprint. Then ask, "How does this hurt us as a team?" and see what your players say. Relate this to the spiritual life, asking, "What areas of your spiritual life are you most likely to cheat on? What impact does this have on your walk with God?"

"This is the love of God, that we keep His commandments."

—1 JOHN 5:3

THE NIKE REVOLUTION

(THE ATHLETE AND OBEDIENCE)

No amount of planning will accomplish a win without execution.

F or over twenty years, Nike has challenged athletes to "Just do it" with their catchy commercials and swoosh logo. The concept has become so ingrained in the American culture that most of us can look at the Nike logo and instantly recall the motivating phrase—"Just do it."

What many people do not know is that Nike was the goddess of victory in Greek mythology. In combining the concepts of victory and just doing it, Nike has now unintentionally provided an excellent illustration of what it means to serve Christ. For the person who claims to follow Jesus, the way to victory is to just do it.

For instance, you can talk about starting a new running routine, but what really matters is when you put on your running shoes, walk out the door, and begin to make progress down the sidewalk or track. As the ancient Chinese proverb states, "The journey of a thousand miles begins with a single step."

While this may appear obvious to those of us who compete in athletic competition, we often miss the parallel to our spiritual lives. Sure, we talk about reading the Bible, praying more, sharing our faith, or serving the poor, but our good intentions often go unrealized. *No amount of planning will accomplish a win without execution.*

God's Word often uses the word "obedience" to refer to things we must do to please God with our lives. For many, the very word "obedience" causes us to cringe. Some people don't want to "obey" anyone. Perhaps this reluctance comes from some past experiences that provided a very poor example of what obedience to God really means. Other people say they have tried to obey, but they just can't do it. These are often people who say they leave church on Sunday excited and ready to go, but then on Monday they return to their everyday habits.

> no amount of planning will accomplish a win without execution.

We don't want to excuse disobedience to God for any reason. Part of our problem is that we often have an inaccurate understanding of true biblical obedience. As a result, we are unable to apply it during our everyday living. An accurate version of obedience is closely related to the new work God has done in our hearts through Christ. Our goal is to live in true obedience in Christ with a "Just do it" attitude.

A New Way of Evaluating

College football controversy stirs every year, as the Bowl Championship Series standings lift certain teams to rankings above what fans think is right while other teams are ranked much lower than expected. The difference is in the way the football teams are evaluated.

When the BCS rankings were first introduced, many believed its computer-calculated efforts would result in far more accurate measurements regarding the Top 25 teams and Bowl Championship selections. Unfortunately, a system based on computer calculations fails to take into consideration certain human factors. Externals such as bad weather, come-from-behind victories, or key injuries remain unmeasured. Even worse, the BCS calculations encourage blowout defeats such as a 62–10 win rather than providing favor to a team that allows playing time to its substitutes after pulling far ahead. In the eyes of many, the definitions hinder the evaluation of which really are the best teams.

Just as in college football, our obedience in following Christ is often hindered due to our standards of evaluation. What we think is best is not always what God teaches as most important. Here are three considerations in developing a proper view of obedience to God.

1. We live for God because He lives in us

Paul wrote, "So then, my beloved, just as you have always obeyed, not as in my presence only, but now much more in my absence, work out your salvation with fear and trembling; for it is God who is at work in you, both to will and to work for His good pleasure" (Philippians 2:12–13).

Many Christians believe we live for God because of fear. Their idea of obedience is the image of a child forced to obey a stern taskmaster standing over him with a whip. Others think of God as a parent who insists on obedience "just because I said so." And some people only obey their bosses, coaches, or other leaders just to stay out of trouble. Instead of an attitude that says "Just do it," they live with a "do it or else" approach.

The Bible gives us a much better definition of obedience, one of doing what you really want to do deep down inside. The element that is missing in so many concepts of obedience is the idea that the desire to obey God is already inside of us. It's like the Gatorade commercial that asks, "Is it in you?" If you are a believer, the answer is yes.

Paul tells us to obey by working out our salvation because of what God has already worked into our new life. Another way to define biblical obedience is simply the working out of what God has worked in. Biblical obedience is joyfully doing on the outside what you really want to do on the inside.

➤ *When is a time you obeyed a coach's instructions even when you wanted to quit or when you questioned his or her directions? How did it make you feel? How is this similar to how many of us think of obeying God? How is it different?*

2. We live for God because our heart desires it

Philippians 2:13 says we can obey because God is at work within us "both to will and to work for His good pleasure." This means we have both the desire and the ability to do what God asks us to do. These are the two components necessary for authentic obedience.

A desire is something you want to do. In fact, the best kind of obedience is always tied to a strong, positive relationship. One way to remember this is with the adage, *Rules without relationship lead to rebellion*. God knows that an intimate relationship is the best way for us to desire obedience to Him. Ultimately, our response will be a delight rather than a duty.

➤ *When do you desire to obey God the most? The least? What makes the difference between the times we most desire to obey God and the times we do not?*

3. We live for God because it increases joy

Jesus said, "Come to Me, all who are weary and heavy-laden, and I will give you rest. Take My yoke upon you and learn from Me, for I am gentle and humble in heart, and you will find rest for your souls. For My yoke is easy and My burden is light" (Matthew 11:28–30).

Does Jesus have a yoke for us that includes obedience? Absolutely. Does He intend it to be a process that defeats and destroys us? Absolutely not. If your load is too heavy for you, bring it to Jesus and let Him show you the joy of following and obeying Him. He might send you help through a fellow believer: "Bear one another's burdens" (Galatians 6:2). Our obedience to Christ should bring us joy rather than a feeling of bondage. A truly obedient Christian life increases joy.

➤ *When you do something that pleases your coach, it usually brings you joy as well. How have you helped bring joy to a coach in your sport? What were the effects on the relationship the two of you had?*

Grab the Water Cooler!

It's a Super Bowl tradition. When the seconds are ticking down and the championship is about to be decided, you can see the players lugging an oversized water jug. They sneak behind the head coach and dump the entire contents of the jug over his head and down his back. On most other days the coach would be furious with his players. Yet on the day the team wins the Super Bowl he actually enjoys the dousing as an overflow of victory.

In 1 John 5:3 the apostle John wrote, "This is the love of God, that we keep His commandments; and His commandments are not burdensome." We prove our love for God by obeying Him. Obedience is the overflow of love, just as the water cooler tradition is an overflow of the Super Bowl celebration.

1. The relationship makes the work worth it

Notice that Jesus did not say, "If you love Me, you better keep My Word." There is no threat here. If we love Jesus, the desire to obey will follow. If the desire to obey is lacking, it's because love is lacking.

Please understand that we should do what is right simply because it is right. Our fundamental problem as Christians is not really obedience. Our problem is keeping our love for Christ vibrant, because love makes our duty a delight.

When Jesus addressed the seven churches in Revelation, He encouraged the church at Ephesus because of its hard work and obedience. Yet He also said, "But I have this against you, that you have left your first love" (Revelation 2:4). In other words, "You don't love Me the way you used to love Me." Christ commanded this church to return to the passionate love they had when first coming to know Him.

➤ *How was your love for Christ when you first trusted in Him? How does it compare with your love for Him now? How can you relate to Christ's words to the church at Ephesus?*

2. The relationship changes everything

John made this critical link when he wrote, "The one who says he abides in Him [Christ] ought himself to walk in the same manner as He walked" (1 John 2:6). To abide is to maintain an intimate relationship. This is the foundation from which obedience flows.

This connection between our love relationship with Christ and our obedience is important because biblical obedience is not a result of being threatened to behave. Instead, it is responding to the desire we already have within us to please God.

When a player feels cared for, the relationship changes everything. When you see a player who struggled on one team traded to another and then suddenly begin to excel, it's often because the player has developed a more positive relationship with the new coach or players on the new team. The same is true with God. God is a caring Coach who provides a relationship that changes everything when it comes to living in obedience.

➤ *Who has been your favorite coach? What did he or she do differently from another coach that made such a difference in your life?*

Watching the X's and O's

The apostle James is an in-your-face kind of guy. He looks right at us and says, "This is the truth. What are you going to do about it?" He is like the coach on the sidelines redrawing the play and shouting, "Pay attention! This is what we must do to win!" He provides four specific ways to improve through paying attention to the X's and O's.

1. Always pay attention to the play

"Everyone must be quick to hear, slow to speak and slow to anger; for the anger of man does not achieve the righteousness of God" (James 1:19–20). He makes it clear that he is talking about being quick to hear God's Word. In other words, the first question we need to ask in any situation is, "What does God say about this in His Word? What play is He calling?"

Along with seeking God's will, James says we need to be slow in our response. By this he means not to react too quickly. We are not supposed to be like the baseball player who attempts to argue every pitch with the umpire. When you learn what God says, don't react with your human anger, because our human nature does not want to obey God. Instead, we need to keep our eyes on the ball, focusing on the game rather than having every call in our favor.

> *When do you find yourself most easily angered? What are some ways you can help yourself respond properly during those times?*

2. Call an audible

Almost all quarterbacks are given each play from the sidelines to run. However, once at the line of scrimmage, the quarterback has the option of running the set play or calling an audible. If he sees that the defense will easily shut down the set play, he can change it to something else that will more likely catch his defenders off guard.

James teaches, "Therefore, putting aside all filthiness and all that remains of wickedness, in humility receive the word implanted, which is able to save your souls" (1:21). The barriers James mentions are general categories for sin in our lives that keep us from obeying God. When we recognize the sin in front of us, we can change our response to avoid the sin and pursue God. The idea behind saving our souls in this verse is not about our salvation, but rather the concept of rescuing us from disaster. Our goal is to make whatever changes are necessary to turn from sin and pursue Christ.

> *What areas of "filthiness" and "wickedness" do you personally have the most trouble avoiding? How could you rearrange your habits to help guard against these areas of temptation?*

3. Make your blocks

The goal of seeing ourselves in God's Word is to become "doers of the word, and not merely hearers who delude themselves" (James 1:22). In other words, we are supposed to do something about what we see, because the Bible is like a mirror that shows you and me how we really look.

The opposite of someone who obeys the Word is the person described in verses 23–24: "For if anyone is a hearer of the word and not a doer, he is like a man who looks at his natural face in a mirror; for once he has looked at himself and gone away, he has immediately forgotten what kind of person he was."

One of the things an offensive line football coach will shout more than anything else is, "Make your blocks!" As offensive linemen, you have very few statistics, so you are usually known for how well you do or do not hit your blocks. Even if you shift correctly for your play, it means nothing if the defending player pushes you aside and makes the tackle.

In the words of James, this means being a doer of the Word rather than just a hearer. What speaks most loudly in life are not our words but our actions. It's like the saying, "How you are acting speaks so loudly I can't hear what you are saying."

James says the Word of God is already written on our hearts. Real spiritual growth happens when the Spirit shows us ourselves and stirs us to act on the Word.

> *What are some areas of life where it is easy to hear the Word but not do the Word? Why are these areas so difficult to practice?*

4. Don't stop until the whistle blows

What we are talking about here requires a response to God's Word that may be different from our norm. The person God blesses is the one who "abides" in His Word. The word "abide" in James 1:25 means to hang out, to stick around. Psalm 1:2 declared that the person who meditates on God's Word "day and night" will be blessed. When you look into the mirror of Scripture, you not only see yourself, but you see what God wants you to become.

In preseason basketball games, you'll often see a player let a loose ball go out of bounds without bothering to dive for it. But during the playoffs, that same loose ball causes players to dive, throw their bodies into the seats, and even perhaps cause themselves injury in order to make the play. Too many Christians live life in the preseason rather than in the playoffs. God wants us to go all out, not letting up near the end of the play.

In football, it's the idea of playing until the whistle blows. When players stop hustling before the play ends, coaches can become furious. Why? Because it shows a lack of desire. James says if we will abide in the Word, looking intently into the law that sets us free and acting on what we see, we will be blessed. Our new nature has been designed to desire God.

Again, with the words of Nike, our calling as Christ's followers is to "just do it." In doing so we will bring about a revolution in our lives that will help us long for obedience to Christ.

takeaway

Faith is something you do, not just something you have. (Faith is both a noun and a verb.)

training points

What must be changed in your life to follow in obedience to Christ? Write down some specific areas you want to adjust, and pray about them together as a group.

31. _____

32. _____

33. _____

transforming others

Who else do I need to pray for on my team or in my life who needs to know Christ and learn to follow Him more closely? Make a list this week and pray for each by name over the next week. Be prepared to share what God does with your group when you meet again.

Is there anyone I need to ask forgiveness from because of my actions against them recently? If so, make a specific plan to contact them this week to discuss this issue. As a group, commit to holding one another accountable to follow through on this action plan.

the coach's perspective

Ask your players, "What is so catchy about the Nike phrase 'Just do it'?" It is simple, direct, and inspiring—but often difficult to do. Then ask, "What types of practices do you try to keep you motivated in your sport?" The same is true spiritually. We love the parts of Scripture that tell us to live out our faith, yet we find it hard to do. Discuss together what practices or even just one practice you could begin as a group to stay motivated in living out your faith. Examples could include a weekly e-mail with prayer requests and encouragement, a time to pray together briefly each day that week at practice, or posting an inspiring Bible verse on your locker.

GROWING THROUGH THE MOTIONS 12

(THE ATHLETE AND MATURITY)

Rookies don't want to be rookies for long.

E very athlete begins as a rookie, but no one wants to be a rookie for long. The same should be true with our spiritual growth. Each step of spiritual growth—from birth to childhood, adolescence, and adulthood—is a stage in the journey of our relationship with Christ, not a final destination. Great athletes are not content to stop right where they are. Likewise, a Christian should never be content with where he or she is spiritually, but always should desire to continue growing in Christ.

Our focus on this session's spiritual journey comes from some amazing words in 1 John, a letter written to help Christians develop a true, life-changing intimacy with God. John stated his goal in the opening verses of his letter:

What was from the beginning, what we have heard, what we have seen with our eyes, what we have looked at and touched with our hands, concerning the Word of Life—and the life was manifested, and we have seen and testify and proclaim to you the eternal life, which was with the Father and was manifested to us—what we have seen and heard we proclaim to you also, so that you too may have fellowship with us; and indeed our fellowship is with the Father, and with His Son Jesus Christ. (1 John 1:1–3)

John's introduction provides a powerful reminder that he had heard and seen and touched Jesus. His message was that he was transferring the truth he learned from Jesus to them. Even though most of his readers had not known Jesus during His time on earth, they could still enjoy the same intimacy with God John knew, because fellowship with God is through the Spirit.

Sometimes people wonder, "Since Jesus isn't here physically as He was with the apostles, how can we know Him personally?" We are not missing out because Jesus is not physically here. In fact, our relationship can actually be more intimate, because when Jesus left, He sent the Holy Spirit to live within us (John 14:17).

From Little League to the Big Leagues

Every athlete has to begin somewhere. In baseball, the first step is often Little League. Starting when they're barely old enough to handle a bat, young boys and girls prove themselves through learning the basic skills of the sport. This league has become so popular that there is even a Little League World Series, complete with teams from across the world competing live on ESPN.

Every Christian has to start somewhere, too. John categorized three specific stages of growth in the process of becoming more like Christ. These stages correspond to the childhood, adolescence, and adulthood in physical life. Each of these stages is important and none of them can be skipped. The early stages of spiritual growth may not take as long as those in our physical growth do, but believers tend to get stuck in one of the early stages along the way that keep them from full maturity in Christ.

We've probably all known a person who is thirty years old in age but only three years old spiritually. This chapter strives to help you identify where you are now and help you move to where you need to be. The goal is to "press on to maturity" (Hebrews 6:1).

1. Big lessons in Little League

The first stage of spiritual development John addresses is the Christian who is in spiritual Little League. John writes, "I am writing to you, little children, because your sins have been forgiven you for His name's sake" (1 John 2:12).

At the end of verse 13 we read, "I have written to you, children, because you know the Father." Young believers know God as their Father, but not in the same intimate way as mature believers.

The original term for "little children" referred to a toddler, so we could also say this is a baby Christian whose spiritual birth was fairly recent. People at this stage of spiritual growth are still learning the basic skills of the game: how to swing a bat and getting the ball from third base to first.

Why does John mention the *forgiveness* of sins as a trait of little children? Because it's basic, a fundamental understanding, something every Christian should know and grasp. They are limited in their understanding, and there is nothing wrong with that if they are truly new to the faith.

Another truth of both Little Leaguers and spiritual children is that they are *dependent on others*. They need someone to show them how to bunt, how to steal second base, and how to catch a fly ball. Spiritual children don't know how to live life yet because they haven't been followers of Christ long enough to know how.

Spiritual childhood is marked by *instability*. Instability depends on circumstances rather than on truth. If things are fine, so are these young Christians. But when times get tough, they are far from fine. They have not yet made the crucial connection between life's problems and spiritual development.

A spiritual Little Leaguer is not a bad stage for someone relatively new to the faith. There is a newness of energy, a freshness of joy, and a desire to learn that motivates those around them. But if you have been a Christian for years and are still completely dependent on someone else to show you how to swing a bat, it is time to grow up.

If you *are* a newer Christian, make sure you are regularly training yourself in the basic skills of the faith through God's Word so you can grow up to have greater impact on those around you.

> ➤ *What were some of the first skills you learned when you first began playing one of your favorite sports as a child? How did learning those first skills affect your athletic abilities later in life? How is this similar to how the basic lessons of our Christian faith influence everything else we do?*

2. Learning to hit a fastball

The apostle John addressed Christians in the second stage of spiritual growth when he wrote, "I am writing to you, young men, because you have overcome the evil one. . . . I have written to you, young men, because you are strong, and the word of God abides in you, and you have overcome the evil one" (1 John 2:13–14).

The names of baseball leagues vary after Little League, but one of the distinct differences in the game played as a teenager is the ability to hit a fastball. In Little League, most pitchers are happy just to get the ball over home plate. With growth, pitchers are able to accelerate in speed and variety of pitches, creating a great distinction between those seriously competing in the game and those just playing for fun.

John calls this stage "young men," though the text of course applies to both men and women. This period of life is marked by conflict and the need to become spiritually strong, learning how to overcome the Devil. At this stage a young person is coming to grips with the realities of the Christian life and begins to encounter his first real competition with the Devil. These are the times in our spiritual journey when we first learn how to use the sword of the Spirit, God's Word, to counter the attacks of the Enemy.

Being a teenager is a tough stage of life. You grow taller, stronger, quicker, and smarter, but you also cope with acne, have more responsibilities, have harder schoolwork, and you might have a job. This phase of life also fosters the most conflict between teenagers and their parents or other authority figures. Instead of accepting everything on blind faith, there are often attempts to challenge what you are told. You feel like moving out and living on your own, but you're not quite ready to handle all of the conditions that come with the move.

During college Jonathan complained about coming home during the summer and holiday breaks because he had to call in at midnight, even though he was now twenty-one. But the rule was that when you live at home, you have to call in at night because I (Tony) am not going to lie awake staring at the ceiling wondering where you are. I at least want to know you're okay.

While young Christians are learning to be strong and overcome Satan with the Word of God, they still need the support and guidance of those further along to help them handle the conflicts, whether they think so or not. Younger believers want to move forward more quickly, thinking they can take on the world and the Devil all by themselves. But they still need help to continue toward greater maturity and development.

If you are in this stage of your spiritual development, there are times when you will fail and be overcome rather than being an overcomer. At those times you will need extra encouragement and mentoring from more mature Christians so you can learn how to avoid the same trap the next time. You also need more specific instruction and training in the Word to sharpen your sword for each increasingly difficult battle.

Learning to hit a fastball as a teenager involves more serious commitment and practice than playing in Little League. So does becoming a more mature follower of Christ. If you are able to use the Word to defeat the Devil, you have grown out of spiritual Little League.

➤ *What are some of the differences between a beginning believer and someone who is more spiritually mature? What rookie mistakes do you discover yourself continuing to make spiritually?*

3. How to handle the big leagues

Every young baseball player dreams of someday playing in the big leagues. Why? Because it represents the highest level of excellence. The goal of spiritual growth is the same—to reach the highest level of excellence as a follower of Christ. John described someone of this maturity as a spiritual father. Twice in chapter 2 he writes, "I am writing to you, fathers, because you know Him who has been from the beginning" (1 John 2:13, 14).

What does it take to play in the major leagues? Years of hard work, near perfection in the fundamentals of the game, and a high degree of success in the areas that count most. Likewise, the fully developed believer knows God at an ever-deeper level that has been pursued over a period of time.

Even a mature believer still needs to grow in Christlikeness because this is a process that lasts a lifetime. There are still many battles with the Enemy to fight and win. The difference a mature follower of Christ models is a quality of depth that can only be gained through the scars of many battles.

We could say the fully developed believer has a personal experience of God's faithfulness and goodness. If you are mature in your faith, you don't require other people telling you how good and faithful God is for you to understand it. Unlike a spiritual child or young man, this person can boldly state, "I know God is real because I have walked with Him all these years and know He is faithful."

But how do you know when you know God intimately? The short answer is that your spirit is able to communicate with God at such a deep level that you pick up signals others often miss.

It's the difference between your average linebacker and All-Pro linebacker Junior Seau. An average linebacker will evaluate the formation in front of him and attempt to shut down the play. Junior's eyes constantly scan the formation, pick up subtle movement from linemen, note the differences in the quarterback's voice, and then he shuts down opposing teams with authority.

When you accepted Christ, your human spirit was drafted to join the Holy Spirit, to be on His team. Over time, the bond you have with Him deepens. A growing and maturing Christian who has been walking with God for many years develops an ever higher level of spiritual awareness. It's what Paul described in 1 Corinthians 2 when he wrote about "things which eye has not seen and ear has not heard, and which have not entered the heart of man, all that God has prepared for those who love Him. For to us God revealed them through the Spirit" (verses 9–10).

Paul was not writing about heaven here, but about the things God reveals to us here on earth. Notice that these are not things we could ever come up with on our own. They are privileges available only through the Holy Spirit, the only One who knows the thoughts of God (1 Corinthians 2:11).

The promise to a person who is listening to the Spirit is that he or she will "know the things freely given to us by God" (1 Corinthians 2:12). These are the things we receive from God through His grace, but we have to be close enough to hear Him speak. It has to do with the intimacy of your walk with God. When God's Word is coming alive for you in ways that change your life and take you in a direction you would never have imagined, **God will increasingly make Himself real to you.** you know what it is like to experience the power of the Holy Spirit, the One who declares to us the Father and the Son who live in us (John 16:13–15).

This puts you in a group of all-stars set apart from the vast majority of the world, including many Christians. In 1 Corinthians 2:14 Paul wrote that the "natural man," or unbeliever, can't grasp anything from God because his spirit is dead. The things of God are "foolishness" to this person.

Even many Christians misunderstand what it truly means to be a mature believer. Spiritually mature believers are so closely connected with God that they think His thoughts after Him.

➤ *Of the three stages discussed (beginner, adolescent, or grown-up), which one would you say best describes you? How would you like to change to continue maturing spiritually?*

Doing Your Part for the Team

Each player on the team has a specific role. A basketball team requires guards, forwards, and a center. A baseball team requires nine players. A football team requires eleven players on the field for every play. As a player, you don't just sit in the bleachers and watch your teammates play. You are either in the game or watching intensely from the sidelines, longing to watch your team come out on top.

As a teammate, you always want to develop to improve your game. God's Word provides us with two practice techniques to prepare us in the process.

1. Do something to grow every day

When you lift weights every day, it's impossible to keep it hidden for long. Pretty soon your teammates and friends start noticing. Why? Because your muscles are growing. As you grow in the grace and knowledge of Christ, your growth will become obvious both to you and to others. God will increasingly make Himself real to you, and your joy will be full as you come to know God more personally through your ongoing development.

At the Last Supper, Philip said to Jesus, "Lord, show us the Father, and it is enough for us" (John 14:8). Jesus answered, "Have I been so long with you, and yet you have not come to know Me, Philip? He who has seen Me has seen the Father" (verse 9).

This conversation shows that it's possible to be a believer and yet not really know God in the way He fully desires. Your goal should be to grow so close to God that whenever you hear or read His Word, it will have your name on it. When you pray, your spirit will discern the Spirit of God revealing the mind and heart of God to you. Relationship fuels development.

➤ *What specific practices have helped you most in your spiritual growth? How have these practices provided the training needed to stand during difficult times?*

2. Do something to help others every day

In addition to developing a heart devoted to God, you must also develop a love for serving others. God lives inside of you to reveal Himself to the world. As His Spirit continues to flame within your heart, spread the fire to others in need of His grace.

You don't have your number retired merely for a great game. You have your number retired for a great career. As God has blessed us, He longs for and expects us to serve as a blessing to others. Jesus also taught His disciples the night before His crucifixion, "By this all men will know that you are My disciples, if you have love for one another" (John 13:35). We must use our lives to show His love to others.

A British runner named Derek Redmon competed in the 1992 Olympics. Midway through his race, he tore a ligament—a very painful injury that sent him to the ground. The rest of the pack ran on to finish the race, but poor Derek just lay there. His dreams, his hopes, and years of training collapsed along with him.

Then, something happened that drew the attention of the crowd and the television cameras away from the winner. Derek pushed himself up off the ground, stood up on wobbly legs, and began making his way around the track. He was determined to finish the race.

After only a few painful strides, it was clear that running was definitely out of the question. He slowed to a walk—a slow, agonizing, tentative walk. Then a man appeared on the track. Security guards tried to deter him, but he was not to be stopped. He put his arm around Derek's shoulder and started helping him make his way toward the finish line. The television commentators quickly confirmed that the man was Jim Redmon, Derek's father. Eventually, father and son crossed the line together while applause thundered throughout the stadium.

In our journey with Christ, the most important thing is not who crosses the finish line first. What matters most is that we continue the race.

We each stumble at times and feel like giving up. That's when our heavenly Father steps out of the stands. Satan may try to stop Him, but our Father will not be deterred. He will wrap His loving arms around us and make sure we finish the race—together.

➤ *In what areas of life are you already helping others? How have you seen God use this to change lives?*

takeaway

It's great to be rookie, but not forever! (Our goal is maturity, not just membership.)

training points

What parts of this study have had the most impact on your personal life? List them below along with applications you would like to take away based on your learning.

34. _____

35. _____

36. _____

transforming others

Who should I share with this week about my commitment to mature in my walk with God?

In what ways can I do something each day this week to help others in need of Christ's love?

the coach's perspective

Ask your players, "What were the things that you found hardest about being new to your team?" This question can apply to their freshman year or the first year at their particular sport. Make the spiritual connection by saying, "Everyone begins as a rookie, but we don't want to stay that way. The same is true in our walk with God." Stress again that becoming a new believer is an amazing transformation, but that ongoing growth is God's requirement and our pleasure. Challenge your players in this final week to live out their faith every day, reminding them of your first week together as you discuss how you want to be remembered after your life is through.

the post-game

Her name was Florence Chadwick. She was a world-class swimmer who had already swum the English Channel. Her next challenge was the twenty-six-mile trek from Catalina Island to the California mainland. Florence entered the water with a number of boats surrounding her as she made the trip. Hour after hour she swam.

Heavy fog dropped the night she attempted her record. As the darkness closed in, she could barely see her hand in front of her face as she stroked. After swimming 15 hours and 55 minutes, she waved to the boats and said, "I can go no farther. I quit."

They hoisted her out of the water and asked, "Why couldn't you keep going?"

She answered, "I couldn't see. The fog blocked me. I felt myself stroking but I couldn't see." After she'd returned to the boat, she discovered she was only a *half mile* from mainland California.

She had worked extremely hard but hadn't reached her goal. Why? She couldn't see. Not a quitter, Florence Chadwick decided to try it again two months later. She jumped in the water. It looked bright and sunny, but after twelve hours darkness and fog rolled in once more. This time the fog was even worse than her previous swim. She couldn't see, but she kept swimming. This time she arrived triumphantly at the California coastline.

Florence was asked, "How did you make it this time?"

She responded, "This time was easy. This time I kept a mental picture of the California coastline in my mind. From the time I left Catalina, I was thinking California coastline. I could see the sand. I could see the beach. I could see the kids swimming. As long as I didn't lose sight of where I was going, I could handle the trip there."

Some of you have quit because you've lost sight. But God says if you keep Him on your mind, you will grow stronger and stronger even though you can't see. Even if everything around you is foggy—relationships, circumstances, money—keep your eyes on God. He will make you a person of influence. He will use you for His glory.

Hall of Fame baseball player Reggie Jackson was known as Mr. October. A member of eleven Division Championships and five World Series titles, his batting average jumped ninety five points in the postseason. His most memorable game came in game six of the 1977 World Series against the Los Angeles Dodgers. On *three consecutive pitches*, he hit three home runs, helping win the clinching game of the series.

When asked why he excelled most during October's postseason play, Reggie Jackson answered, "Because I begin the season with the postseason in mind." What fueled Reggie's postseason should fuel our lives as well. As Christians, we know we have eternity ahead of us, endless worship in the presence of Jesus Christ. As you seek to "get in the game," live with our eternity in mind, allowing it to fuel your daily life and actions.

As we pursue the life of our ultimate Head Coach, Jesus Christ, we will continually and progressively grow in our faith. We will become spiritual athletes who give our all for our Savior. No Super Bowl, no NCAA Championship, no World Series, nor any other title could ever compare with such a victory. Stand strong. Get in the game and become an athlete fully following Jesus Christ.

about the authors

Dr. Tony Evans, the first African-American to graduate with a doctoral degree from Dallas Theological Seminary, is senior pastor of the 7,000-member Oak Cliff Bible Fellowship and president of The Urban Alternative, a national organization that seeks to bring about spiritual renewal in urban America. He has served as chaplain for the Dallas Cowboys and Dallas Mavericks. His radio broadcast, *The Alternative,* can be heard on more than 500 stations daily throughout the United States and worldwide. Tony and his wife, Lois, have four children and four grandchildren and live in Dallas, Texas.

Jonathan Evans is the son of Dr. Tony Evans and a former standout fullback at Baylor University. He is currently signed to an NFL team. A frequent communicator on living out your faith as an athlete, Jonathan is committed to developing the next generation of devoted Christian athletes.

Dillon Burroughs is a freelance writer and graduate of Dallas Theological Seminary. He has written for numerous Christian publications including *Leadership Journal, Group Magazine,* and *Discipleship Journal.* Dillon lives with his wife, Deborah, and children Ben and Natalie in Indianapolis, Indiana.

For More Information on the Author's Ministries:

www.tonyevans.org

1-800-800-3222